THE GLOBE SECTION 1

6

1

6

5

11

11

5

10

14

17

14

16

24

16

24

22

27

22

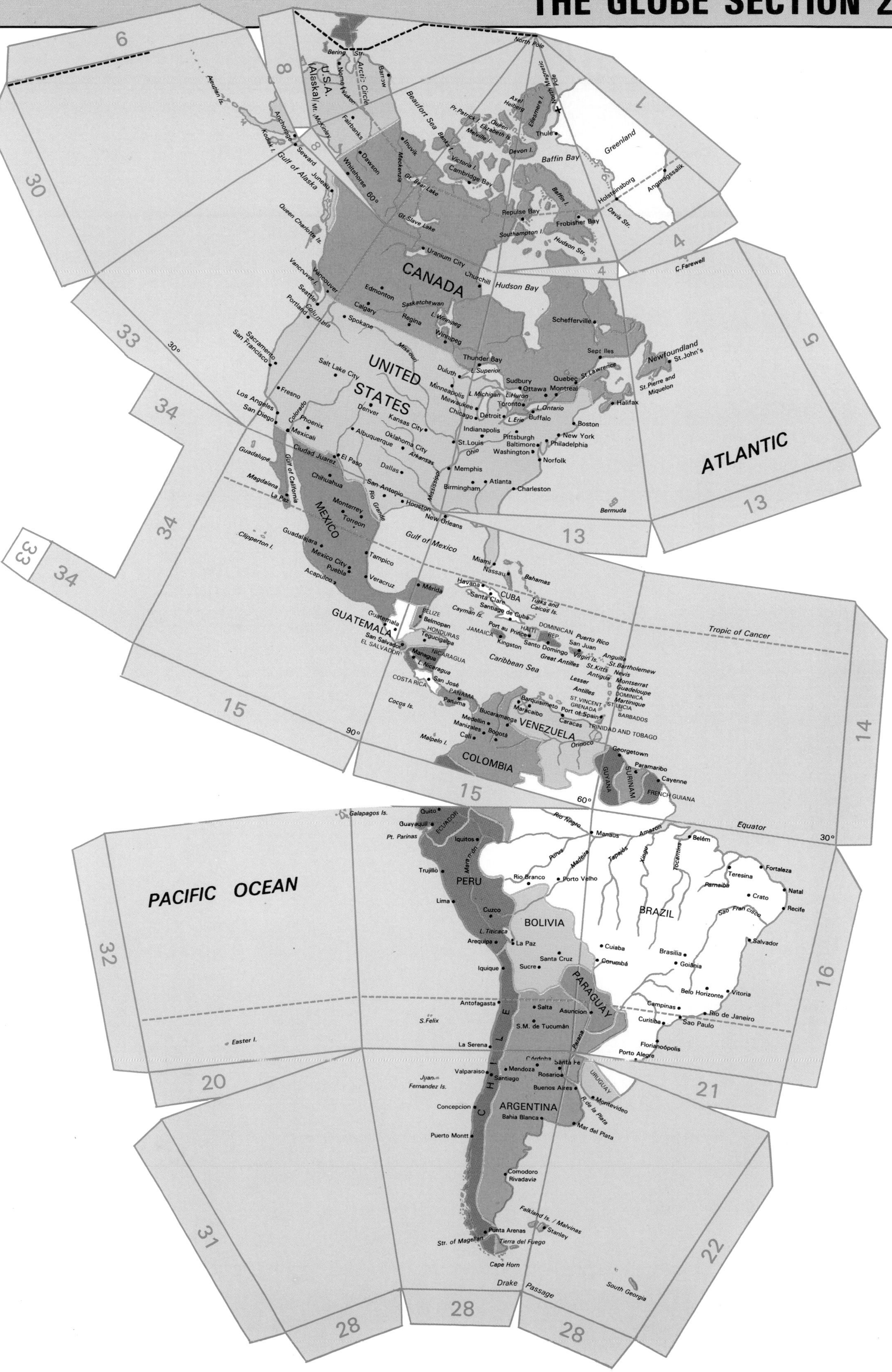
6
8
U.S.A. (Alaska)
Bering Str.
Arctic Circle
Nome
Yukon
Mt. McKinley
Barrow
North Pole
Aleutian Is.
Anchorage
Kodiak I.
Seward
Gulf of Alaska
Juneau
Fairbanks
Beaufort Sea
Banks I.
Pr. Patrick
Queen Elizabeth Is.
Melville I.
Axel Heiberg
Ellesmere I.
North Magnetic Pole
Thule
Devon I.
Greenland
7
Baffin Bay
Angmagssalik
Holsteinsborg
Davis Str.
Baffin I.
Inuvik
Mackenzie
Dawson
Whitehorse
Victoria I.
Cambridge Bay
Gt. Bear Lake
60°
30
Queen Charlotte Is.
Gt. Slave Lake
Repulse Bay
Southampton I.
Frobisher Bay
Hudson Str.
4
Uranium City
CANADA
Churchill
Hudson Bay
C. Farewell
Vancouver I.
Vancouver
Seattle
Columbia
Portland
Edmonton
Calgary
Saskatchewan
Regina
L. Winnipeg
Winnipeg
Spokane
Schefferville
33
30°
Sacramento
San Francisco
Missouri
Salt Lake City
UNITED STATES
Thunder Bay
Duluth
L. Superior
Sept Iles
Newfoundland
St. John's
St. Pierre and Miquelon
5
Quebec
St. Lawrence
Sudbury
Ottawa
Montreal
Halifax
Minneapolis
Milwaukee
L. Michigan
L. Huron
Toronto
L. Ontario
Fresno
34
Los Angeles
San Diego
Colorado
Phoenix
Mexicali
Denver
Kansas City
Chicago
Detroit
L. Erie
Buffalo
Boston
Indianapolis
Pittsburgh
Baltimore
New York
Philadelphia
Washington
Albuquerque
Oklahoma City
St. Louis
Ohio
Arkansas
Norfolk
ATLANTIC
Guadalupe
Ciudad Juarez
El Paso
Dallas
Memphis
Gulf of California
Chihuahua
Mississippi
Atlanta
Birmingham
Charleston
Magdalena
La Paz
San Antonio
Rio Grande
Houston
MEXICO
Monterrey
Torreon
Bermuda
13
New Orleans
Gulf of Mexico
Clipperton I.
Guadalajara
Tampico
Mexico City
Puebla
Acapulco
Veracruz
Miami
Nassau
Bahamas
Mérida
Havana
Santa Clara
CUBA
Santiago de Cuba
Turks and Caicos Is.
Cayman Is.
Tropic of Cancer
GUATEMALA
Guatemala
BELIZE
Belmopan
HONDURAS
Tegucigalpa
JAMAICA
Kingston
Port au Prince
HAITI
DOMINICAN REP.
Santo Domingo
Puerto Rico
San Juan
San Salvador
EL SALVADOR
NICARAGUA
Managua
L. Nicaragua
Caribbean Sea
Great Antilles
Virgin Is.
Anguilla
St. Bartholemew
St. Kitts
Nevis
Antigua
Montserrat
Guadeloupe
Dominica
Martinique
St. Lucia
Lesser Antilles
St. Vincent
Grenada
Barbados
COSTA RICA
San José
PANAMA
Panama
Cocos Is.
Barquisimeto
Maracaibo
Port of Spain
Caracas
Trinidad and Tobago
Bucaramanga
Medellín
Manizales
Bogotá
Cali
VENEZUELA
Orinoco
15
90°
Malpelo I.
COLOMBIA
Georgetown
Paramaribo
Cayenne
GUYANA
SURINAM
FRENCH GUIANA
14
60°
Galapagos Is.
Quito
Guayaquil
ECUADOR
Pt. Parinas
Iquitos
Marañón
Rio Negro
Manaus
Amazon
Belém
Equator
30°
Purus
Madeira
Tapajós
Xingu
Tocantins
Fortaleza
Teresina
Parnaiba
Crato
Natal
Recife
Trujillo
PERU
Rio Branco
Porto Velho
BRAZIL
São Francisco
PACIFIC OCEAN
Lima
Cuzco
BOLIVIA
L. Titicaca
Arequipa
La Paz
Salvador
Cuiaba
Corumbá
Brasilia
Goiânia
32
Santa Cruz
Sucre
Iquique
PARAGUAY
16
Belo Horizonte
Vitoria
Antofagasta
Salta
Asuncion
Campinas
Rio de Janeiro
S. Felix
S.M. de Tucumán
CHILE
Curitiba
São Paulo
Paraná
Easter I.
La Serena
Florianópolis
Porto Alegre
Córdoba
Santa Fe
20
Valparaiso
Mendoza
Santiago
Rosario
URUGUAY
21
Juan Fernandez Is.
Buenos Aires
ARGENTINA
Montevideo
R. de la Plata
Concepcion
Bahia Blanca
Mar del Plata
Puerto Montt
Comodoro Rivadavia
31
Falkland Is. / Malvinas
Punta Arenas
Stanley
22
Str. of Magellan
Tierra del Fuego
Cape Horn
Drake Passage
South Georgia
28

20 21

15 15

13

13

33

4 4

8

8

3

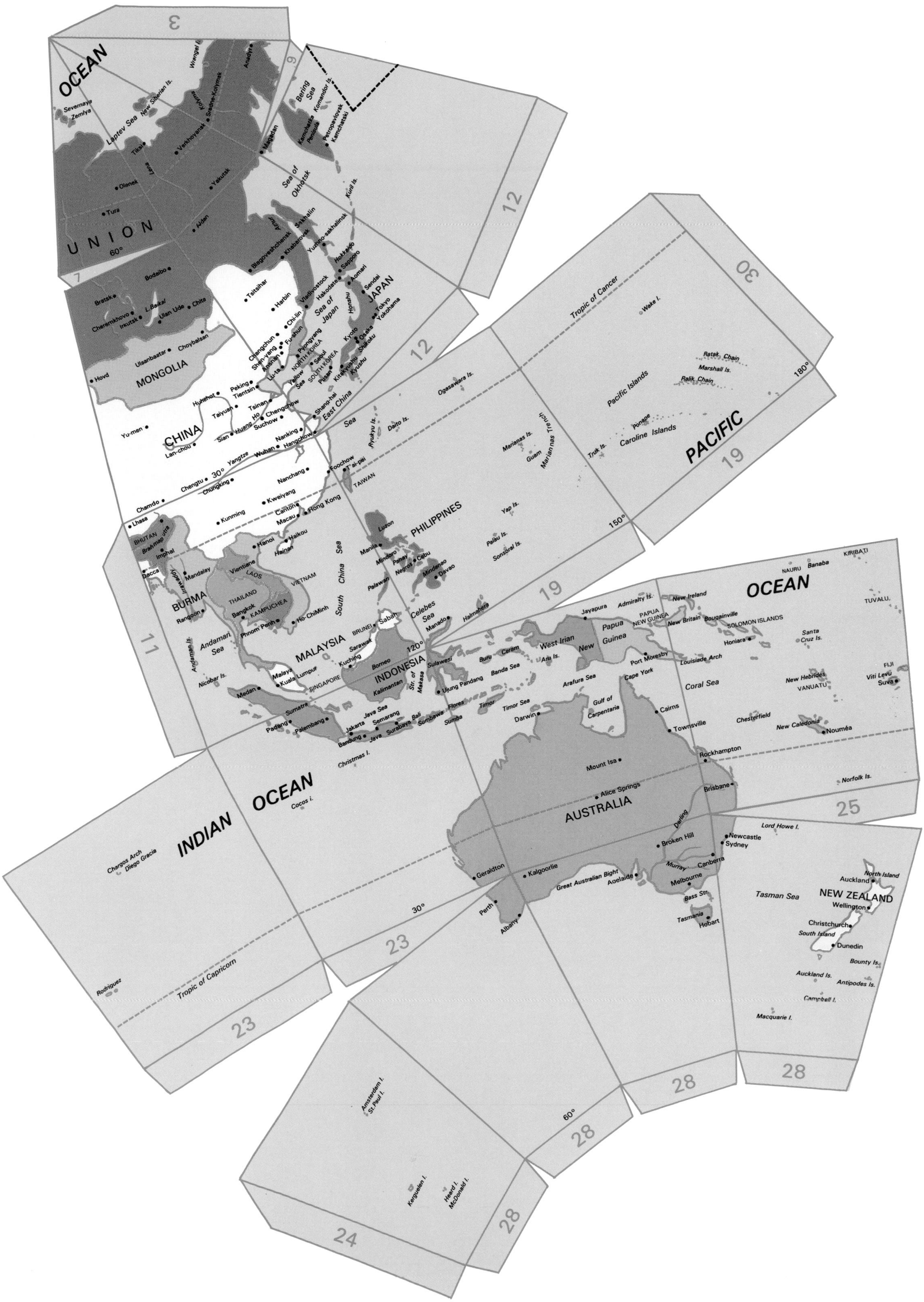
OCEAN
UNION
60°
Severnaya Zemlya
Laptev Sea
New Siberian Is.
Wrangel I.
Anadyr
Tiksi
Verkhoyansk
Sredne-Kolymsk
Kolyma
Lena
Olenek
Yakutsk
Tura
Aldan
Magadan
Bering Sea
Komandor Is.
Kamchatka Peninsula
Petropavlovsk Kamchatski
Sea of Okhotsk
Kuril Is.
Amur
Sakhalin
Blagoveshchensk
Khabarovsk
Yuzhno-sakhalinsk
Hokkaido
Sapporo
Aomori
Sendai
JAPAN
Honshu
Tokyo
Yokohama
Kyoto
Osaka
Shikoku
Kyushu
Kitakyushu
Hakodate
Vladivostok
Sea of Japan
Bodaibo
Bratsk
Cheremkhovo
Irkutsk
L. Baikal
Ulan Ude
Chita
Tsitsihar
Harbin
Chi-lin
Changchun
Shen-yang
Fu-shun
Anshan
Lu-ta
Pyongyang
NORTH KOREA
Seoul
SOUTH KOREA
Pusan
Yellow Sea
Ulaanbaatar
Choybalsan
Hovd
MONGOLIA
Huhehot
Peking
Tientsin
Taiyuan
Tsinan
Huang Ho
Chengchow
Suchow
Sian
Shang-hai
East China Sea
Yu-men
CHINA
Lan-chou
Nanking
Hangchow
Wuhan
Yangtze
30°
Chengtu
Chungking
Nanchang
Foochow
T'ai-pei
TAIWAN
Chamdo
Lhasa
Kunming
Kweiyang
Canton
Macau
Hong Kong
BHUTAN
Brahmaputra
Imphal
Dacca
Hanoi
Haikou
Hainan
Mandalay
Vientiane
LAOS
VIETNAM
THAILAND
BURMA
Irrawaddy
Rangoon
Bangkok
KAMPUCHEA
Phnom Penh
Ho-ChiMinh
South China Sea
Andaman Sea
Andaman Is.
Nicobar Is.
MALAYSIA
Malaya
Kuala Lumpur
SINGAPORE
BRUNEI
Sabah
Sarawak
Kuching
Borneo
Kalimantan
INDONESIA
Medan
Sumatra
Padang
Palembang
Jakarta
Bandung
Java Sea
Semarang
Java
Surabaya
Bali
Sumbawa
Flores
Sumba
Timor
Christmas I.
Luzon
PHILIPPINES
Manila
Mindoro
Panay
Negros
Cebu
Palawan
Mindanao
Davao
Celebes Sea
Manado
Halmahera
Sulawesi
Str. of Makasa
Ujung Pandang
Buru
Ceram
Banda Sea
Aru Is.
Timor Sea
Arafura Sea
Darwin
Gulf of Carpentaria
Ryukyu Is.
Daito Is.
Ogasawara Is.
Marianas Is.
Guam
Marianas Trench
Yap Is.
Palau Is.
Sonsoral Is.
150°
Tropic of Cancer
Wake I.
Pacific Islands
Ratak Chain
Marshall Is.
Ralik Chain
Ponape
Truk Is.
Caroline Islands
PACIFIC
180°
NAURU
Banaba
KIRIBATI
OCEAN
TUVALU
Jayapura
Admiralty Is.
New Ireland
New Britain
Bougainville
PAPUA NEW GUINEA
SOLOMON ISLANDS
West Irian
New Guinea
Papua
Port Moresby
Louisiade Arch
Honiara
Santa Cruz Is.
FIJI
Viti Levu
Suva
New Hebrides
VANUATU
Cape York
Coral Sea
Cairns
Townsville
Chesterfield
New Caledonia
Nouméa
Rockhampton
Mount Isa
Alice Springs
Brisbane
Norfolk Is.
AUSTRALIA
Darling
Broken Hill
Newcastle
Sydney
Lord Howe I.
Murray
Canberra
Melbourne
Adelaide
Great Australian Bight
Kalgoorlie
Geraldton
Perth
Albany
Bass Str.
Tasmania
Hobart
Tasman Sea
North Island
Auckland
NEW ZEALAND
Wellington
Christchurch
South Island
Dunedin
Bounty Is.
Auckland Is.
Antipodes Is.
Campbell I.
Macquarie I.
INDIAN
OCEAN
Cocos I.
Chagos Arch
Diego Garcia
30°
Rodriguez
Tropic of Capricorn
Amsterdam I.
St. Paul I.
60°
Kerguelen I.
Heard I.
McDonald I.
3
6
7
12
12
30
19
19
11
25
23
23
23
28
28
28
28
28
24

23

18 23 29

18 25

29

19

19

7 12

7 12

2

9 9

HOW TO MAKE THE MINIBOOK

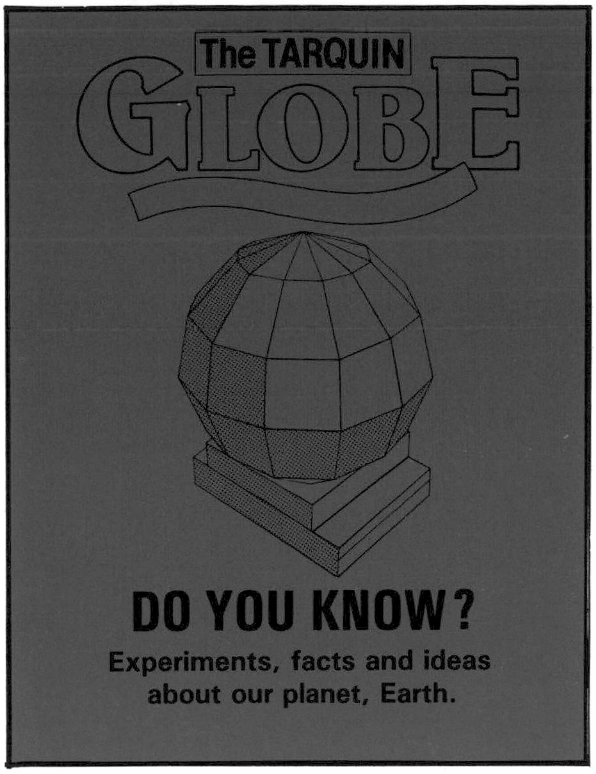

The TARQUIN
GLOBE
DO YOU KNOW?
Experiments, facts and ideas about our planet, Earth.

1. Remove the six pages which make the minibook.
2. Score along the lines marked ▶———◀
3. Cut out precisely.
4. Fold away from you to make a hill fold.
5. Assemble the six sections to make the 24 page minibook.

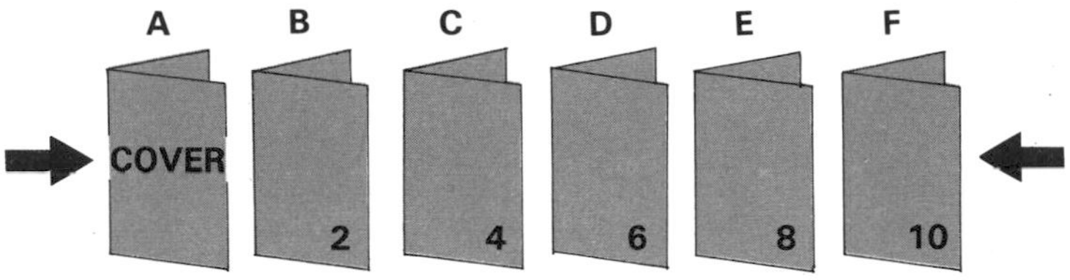

Do a careful check that the pages are in the correct order.

6. Fix them together. If you have a suitable stapler, then that is probably the easiest way. Otherwise use a needle and thread like the bookbinders of old!
7. Store the minibook in the stand drawer.

EXPERIMENTS WITH DISTANCE AND TIME

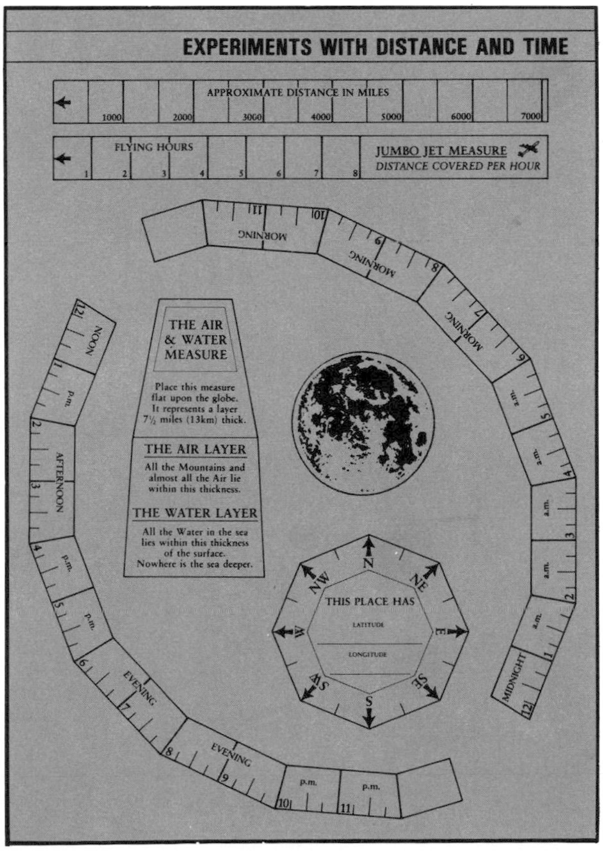

1. Cut out the page from the book.
2. Score along all the lines marked — — SCORE — —
3. Cut out all the pieces precisely.
4. Fold away from you along the score lines to make hill folds. Crease firmly.
5. Glue together the two halves of the time collar. It will fit snugly on your globe at latitude 30°. By turning it you can find the time anywhere.

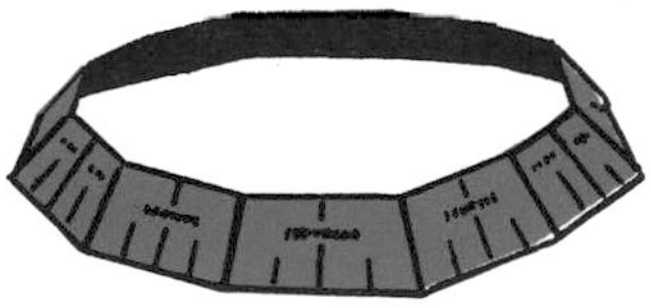

6. Store the pieces in the stand drawer until you need them.

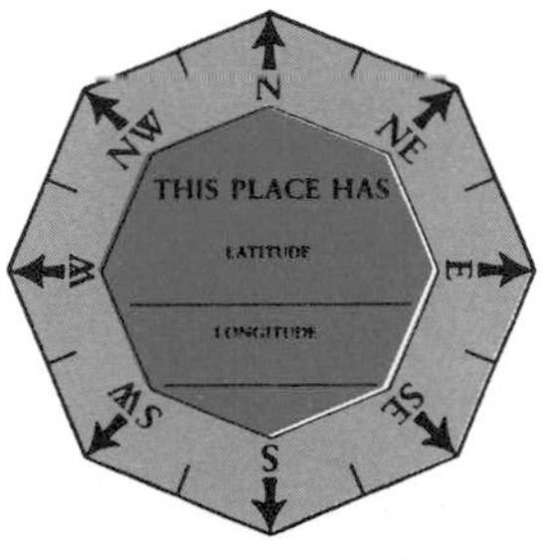

You might like to fix this compass plaque on to a window sill or built-in horizontal surface and so maintain a permanent reminder of directions.

NEW PERSPECTIVES

One benefit of a globe is that it gives us a different viewpoint for thinking about the Earth and our own position on it. It is almost as if we are outside ourselves, looking from space at a planet which we remember in a quite different way. Such a change of perspective allows us to make sense of many mysteries and explain things which would otherwise be most confusing. Why does the Sun cross the sky during the day? Why is there day and night? Why is there summer and winter? Why is the Sun higher in the sky at certain times of the year rather than others? Our ancestors lived for generation after generation quite unable to explain phenomena which we can understand today with ease. But how clever some of the early thinkers were to make use of events and observations which most people would scarcely notice.

There is a remarkable story of an Ancient Greek called Eratosthenes who was in Aswan in Egypt. One day he looked down a deep well and saw the Sun's disc reflected in the water at the bottom. Most of us would be surprised by this, but think no more of it.Eratosthenes was however different. He immediately realised that because it was a deep well, the Sun must be directly overhead, something he knew never happened in Alexandria where he usually lived. From this he was able to work out that the Earth was a sphere and to calculate its circumference to a remarkable degree of accuracy. He calculated that it was 24,662 miles (39,459km). In the direction he measured it the true length was 24,819 miles (39,710km). There was an element of good fortune in getting an answer so close to the real one, but this story shows the power of taking a viewpoint outside the ordinary.

It is a curious fact that the knowledge of Eratosthenes was completely lost and in the middle ages many people believed that the Earth was flat. It was feared that if you sailed too far from land, then you would fall over the edge. Columbus was one of those who believed that the Earth was a sphere and that by sailing west he could reach India. However, his estimation of the size of the Earth was far too low and so when he arrived in the West Indies and discovered the Americas he thought he had reached India. Because of that error, the native peoples of America are still called 'Indians', although we usually say 'Red Indians' or 'Amerindians' to distinguish them from the inhabitants of India itself. Later explorers discovered the Pacific Ocean and the true size of the Earth became known again. The distance between the Caribbean and India cannot be ignored!

The world is a fascinating place to explore. Either by thought and imagination as Eratosthenes did so successfully without needing to leave Egypt, or by travelling the world as many others have done.It is hoped that this oddly shaped globe, the ideas put forward in the minibook and the simple experiments can give you a new perspective and a new understanding of our planet. If this is true, then we shall have succeeded in our aim.

HOME-FACTS

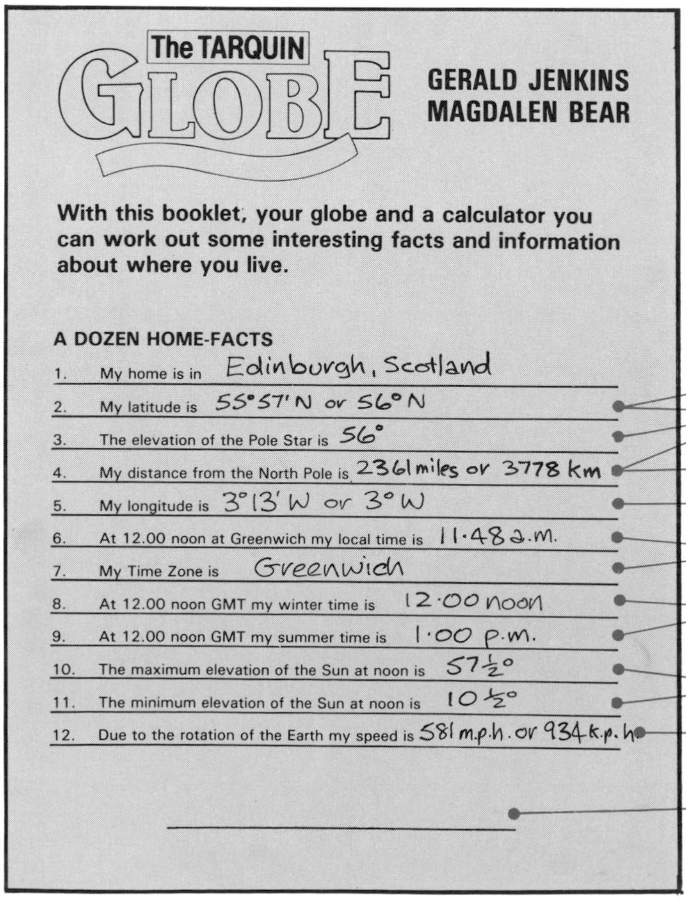

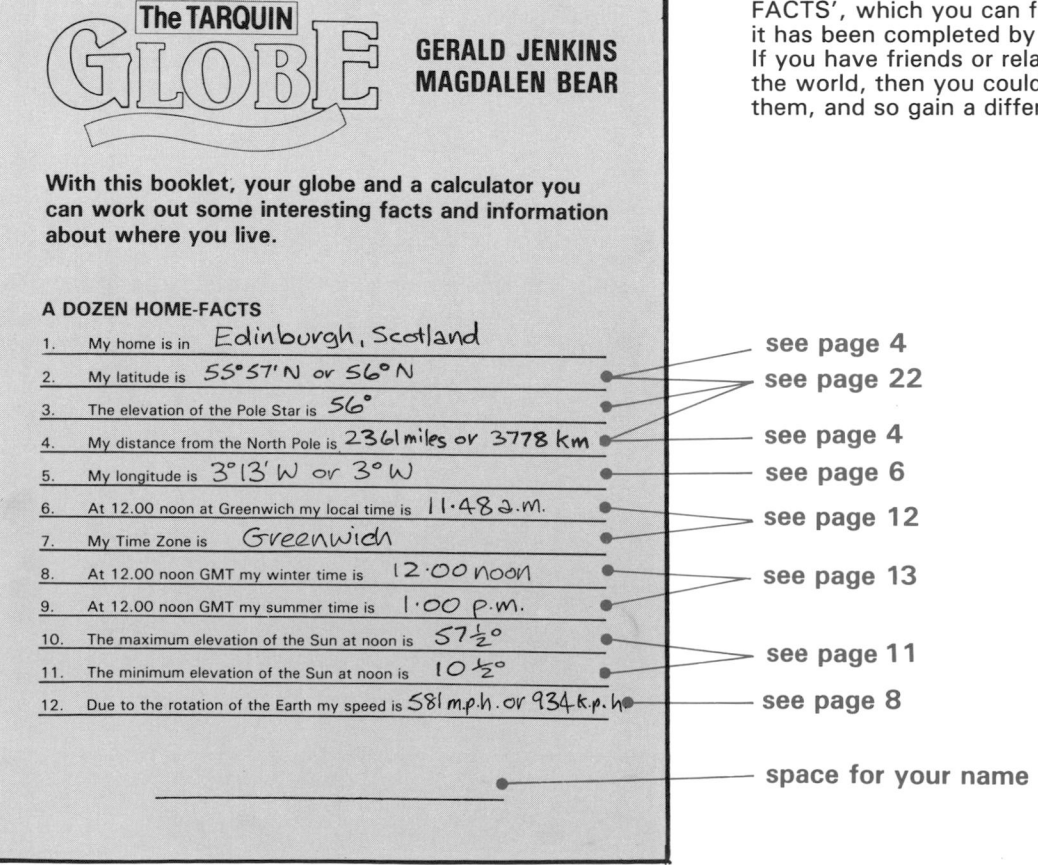

The TARQUIN GLOBE

GERALD JENKINS
MAGDALEN BEAR

With this booklet, your globe and a calculator you can work out some interesting facts and information about where you live.

A DOZEN HOME-FACTS

1. My home is in Edinburgh, Scotland
2. My latitude is 55°57' N or 56° N
3. The elevation of the Pole Star is 56°
4. My distance from the North Pole is 2361 miles or 3778 km
5. My longitude is 3°13' W or 3° W
6. At 12.00 noon at Greenwich my local time is 11·48 a.m.
7. My Time Zone is Greenwich
8. At 12.00 noon GMT my winter time is 12·00 noon
9. At 12.00 noon GMT my summer time is 1·00 p.m.
10. The maximum elevation of the Sun at noon is 57½°
11. The minimum elevation of the Sun at noon is 10½°
12. Due to the rotation of the Earth my speed is 581 m.p.h. or 934 k.p.h.

see page 4
see page 22
see page 4
see page 6
see page 12
see page 13
see page 11
see page 8

space for your name

In the minibook you will find a page devoted to 'HOME-FACTS', which you can fill in wherever you live. On the left it has been completed by someone who lives in Edinburgh. If you have friends or relatives who live in other parts of the world, then you could also work out the answers for them, and so gain a different perspective.

EXPERIMENTS WITH DISTANCE AND TIME

APPROXIMATE DISTANCE IN MILES

← 1000 2000 3000 4000 5000 6000 7000

FLYING HOURS

← 1 2 3 4 5 6 7 8

JUMBO JET MEASURE

DISTANCE COVERED PER HOUR

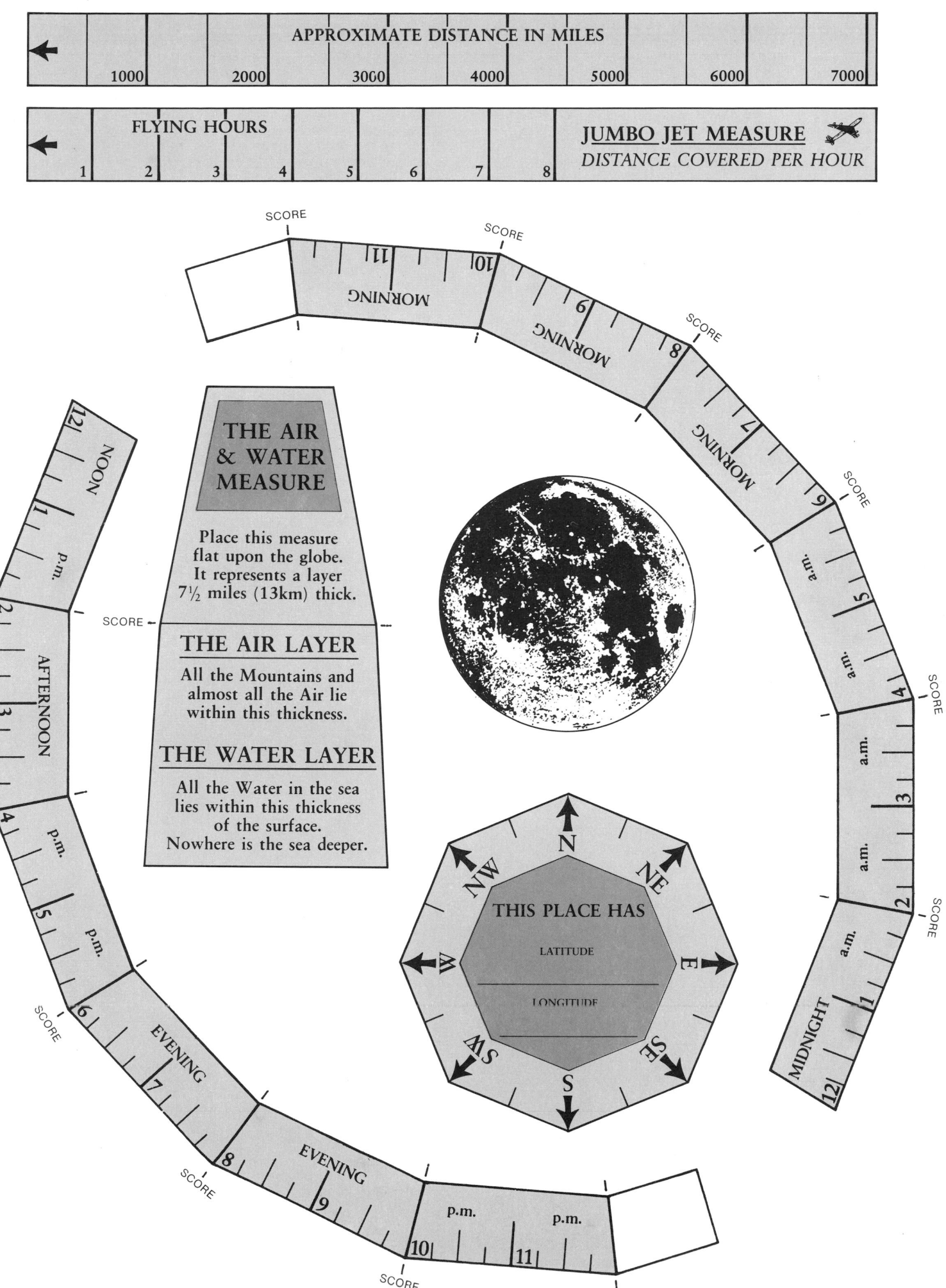

SCORE

MORNING 11 10

SCORE

MORNING 9 8

SCORE

MORNING 7 6

SCORE

a.m. 5 a.m. 4

SCORE

a.m. 3 a.m. 2

SCORE

a.m. 1 MIDNIGHT 12

12 NOON 1 p.m.

SCORE

2 AFTERNOON 3

SCORE

4 p.m. 5 p.m.

SCORE

6 EVENING 7

SCORE

8 EVENING 9

p.m. 10 p.m. 11

SCORE

SCORE

THE AIR & WATER MEASURE

Place this measure flat upon the globe. It represents a layer 7½ miles (13km) thick.

SCORE

THE AIR LAYER

All the Mountains and almost all the Air lie within this thickness.

THE WATER LAYER

All the Water in the sea lies within this thickness of the surface. Nowhere is the sea deeper.

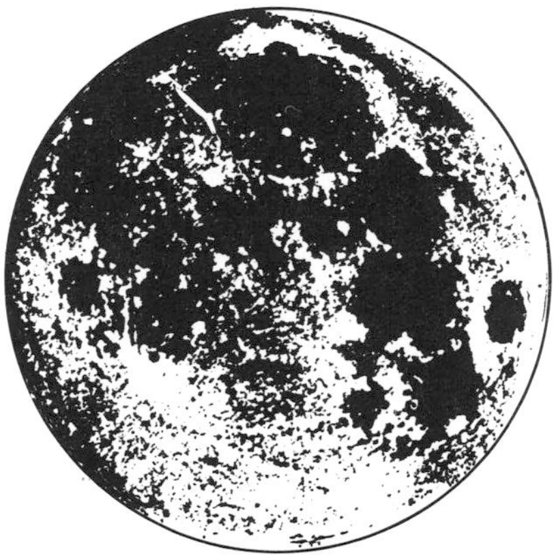

N NE E SE S SW W NW

THIS PLACE HAS

LATITUDE

LONGITUDE

APPROXIMATE DISTANCE IN KILOMETRES

1000 2000 3000 4000 5000 6000 7000 8000 9000 10,000

OCEAN LINER MEASURE

DISTANCE COVERED PER DAY

CRUISING DAYS

1 2 3 4 5 6 7 8 9

FULL MOON

This disc is to the same scale as the Tarquin globe. In proportion it should be held 19 feet or 5.80 metres away from the globe.

The TARQUIN GLOBE

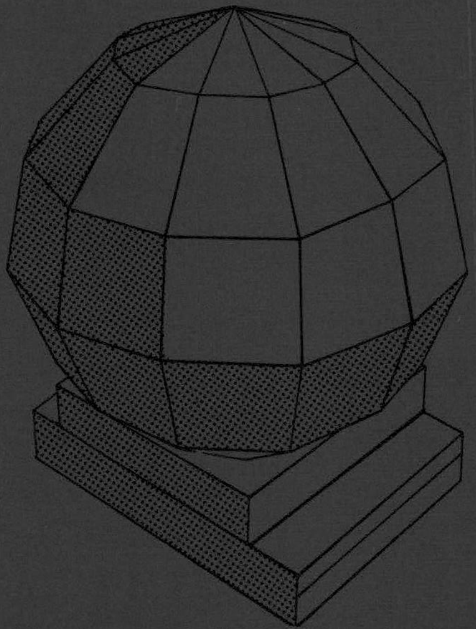

DO YOU KNOW?

Experiments, facts and ideas about our planet, Earth.

TARQUIN PUBLICATIONS 0 906212 55 3

STRADBROKE DISS NORFOLK. IP21 5JP
TEL. 037 984 218

The TARQUIN GLOBE

GERALD JENKINS
MAGDALEN BEAR

With this booklet, your globe and a calculator you can work out some interesting facts and information about where you live.

A DOZEN HOME-FACTS

1. My home is in ______
2. My latitude is ______
3. The elevation of the Pole Star is ______
4. My distance from the North Pole is ______
5. My longitude is ______
6. At 12.00 noon at Greenwich my local time is ______
7. My Time Zone is ______
8. At 12.00 noon GMT my winter time is ______
9. At 12.00 noon GMT my summer time is ______
10. The maximum elevation of the Sun at noon is ______
11. The minimum elevation of the Sun at noon is ______
12. Due to the rotation of the Earth my speed is ______

WHERE DOES THE EARTH'S AXIS POINT ?

During the night all the stars seem to rotate about a fixed point. This apparent movement is due to the rotation of the Earth and the fixed point marks the place in the sky directly above the pole. In the northern sky there is a bright star close to the fixed point and it is called 'Polaris' or 'The Pole Star'. In the southern sky, the 'Southern Cross' is close to the fixed point, but there is no bright star actually there.

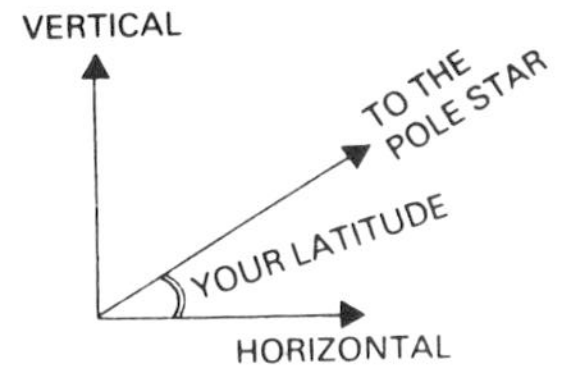

In the northern hemisphere the Pole Star is always due north of where you are and its angle of elevation is always the same as your latitude.

You can set up an instrument to measure your latitude at any time of night throughout the year. The answer is always the same.

A REMARKABLE EXPERIMENT

The flattened nature of your globe does make a simple and impressive experiment possible.

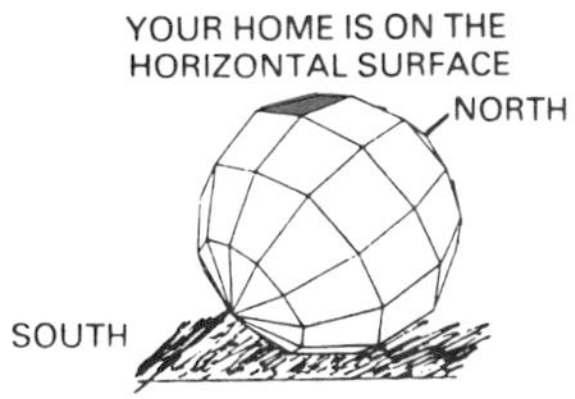

(1) Place it on a table in sunlight so that the flattened surface which contains your home is horizontal. It will then be the highest surface.

(2) Turn it so the axis is aligned north-south. If you use a compass, see page 5 and allow for the magnetic variation.

Now your globe is parallel to the real Earth and both axes point to the Pole Star whether you can see it or not. The real sunlight is now falling on your globe just as the real sunlight is falling on the real Earth. You can see where it is day, where it is night and where the Sun is directly overhead, now, at this minute.

You can even use a pencil or a spent match to see how trees in various countries are casting their shadows - now! See how the shadows are different north or south of the Equator or where it is morning or late afternoon.

Try this experiment at different times of the day and at different times of the year but don't leave your globe in the sunlight for too long or it will begin to fade.

In the southern hemisphere the globe would rest on the table in the position shown on the right. The axis would still point to the Pole Star, but downwards, through the Earth itself.

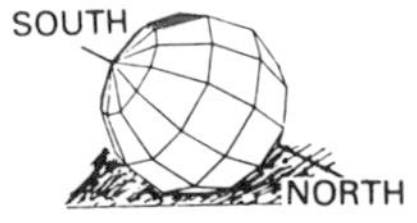

WHICH WAY IS THE CENTRE OF THE EARTH ?

This is a very easy question to answer wherever you are. The answer is downwards, down beneath your feet. In fact the word 'down' really means 'towards the centre of the Earth'. The word 'up' really means 'away from the centre of the Earth'.

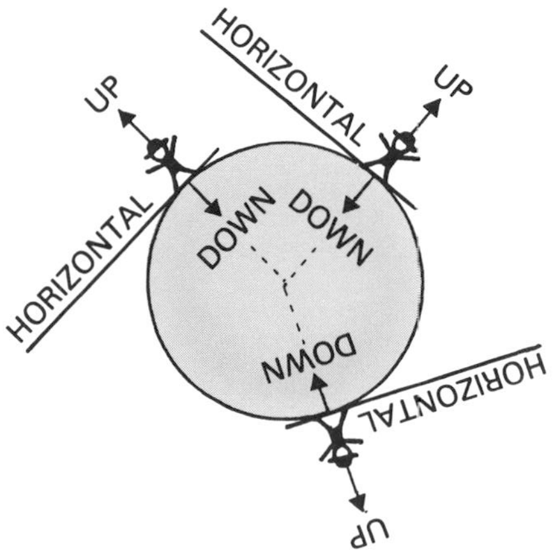

The force of gravity acts directly towards the centre of the Earth and this is the direction we call vertical. Builders use a plumb line to make sure that walls are vertical and will not tilt and collapse. They also use a spirit level to make other surfaces horizontal. Horizontal is the direction at right angles to vertical at every point on the Earth's surface. Ignoring the waves, the sea is horizontal at every point on the globe.

A GREAT BORE !

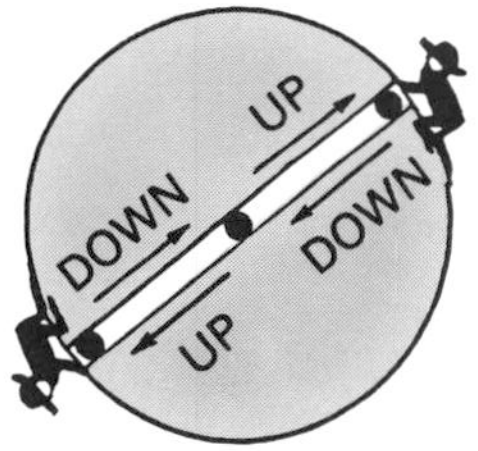

Suppose we were to bore a hole right through the centre of the Earth and out the other side. What would happen?

Ignore the fact that it would be completely impossible. Just a few kilometres under the surface the rocks are enormously hot and under huge pressure. Deeper still, the whole core of the Earth may be molten iron and nickel. Let us ignore all that!

Now we have our imaginary hole, let us drop a cannon ball down it. It would fall downwards, accelerating all the time until it was going very fast indeed. Once it had passed the centre it would be going upwards and so would begin to slow down. It would stop just as it reached the surface at the other end.

If no-one grabbed it, then it would fall back down the hole and not stop until it reached the surface on the other side. If no-one grabbed it, then........ Could this be used for the fastest Post Office service ever for letters which do not burn or melt?

Use your globe to find possible places where such a hole could be bored so that it was on land at both ends. What about Brazil - The Philippines, Hawaii - Botswana or Greenland - Antarctica. Can you find any others?

THE EARTH IS A SPHERE - WELL, ALMOST !

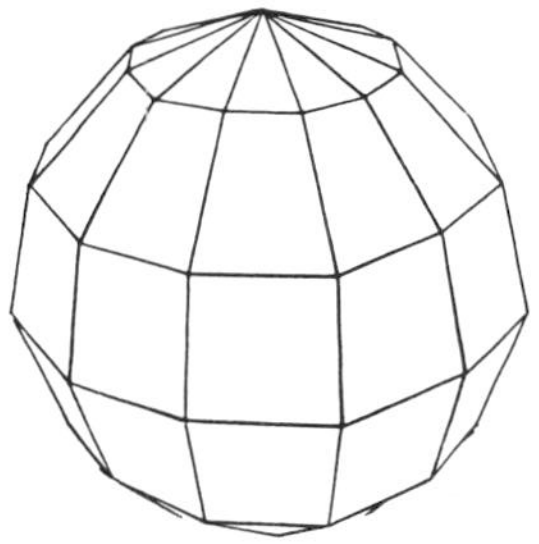

You may be surprised at first by the shape of this globe. The Earth itself is very close to being a perfect sphere and so it may seem curious to design and make a globe which is at first sight a rather odd shape.
A true sphere cannot be made from flat card and so any cardboard globe must be an approximation. Many different shapes could have been chosen, but this one does have some special advantages. It makes use of the 30° circles of latitude and longitude and each corner does lie on the true sphere. The shape has been obtained by smoothing off the curvature between those points. Of course this does alter the shape of the countries a little, but if you compare it with a 'proper' globe, you will see that the distortion is very small.

Distortion in map making is always inevitable, because the pages of an Atlas are flat and the surface of the Earth is curved. The type of distortion used by map makers is called a 'projection'. If you look through an atlas you will see that different projections are used for different purposes. You will see names like 'Mercator's Projection', 'Conic Projection', Bonne Projection' etc.

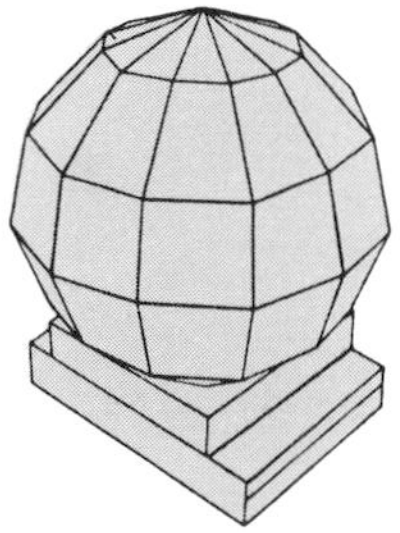

You should think of your Tarquin Globe as a kind of three-dimensional atlas which uses a special projection to give a very useful and convenient way of looking at our three-dimensional world. The scale is approximately 1030 miles to the inch or 650 kilometres to the centimetre.

WHERE IS THE EARTH'S AXIS ?

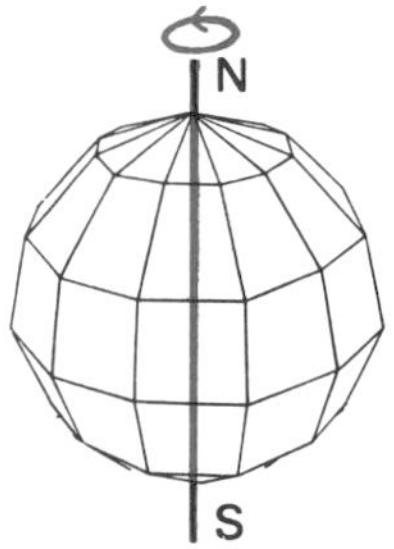

The folds on your globe converge to two very special points on the Earth, the North Pole and the South Pole. The Earth spins about an axis through these two points.

If you go to the North or South Pole you will see no direct evidence that the mighty Earth is spinning about these places. Explorers have to make very careful astronomical observations to be sure that they have reached their goal.

WHAT DO THE FOLDS REPRESENT ?

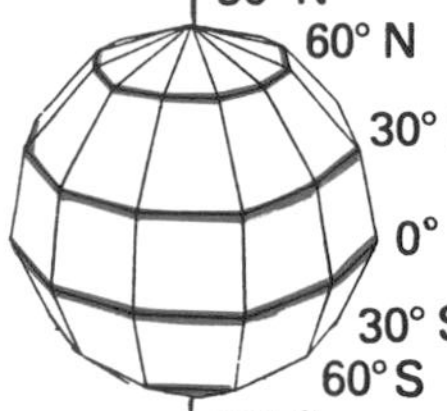

The folds at right angles to the axis are called circles of latitude. On our globe they are not circles but 12 sided polygons, but the difference is small.

The largest circle of latitude is the Equator which is called 0°. The other circles are 30° and 60° North and South. The North Pole is 90°N and the South Pole 90°S.

The centre of each circle of latitude is on the axis.

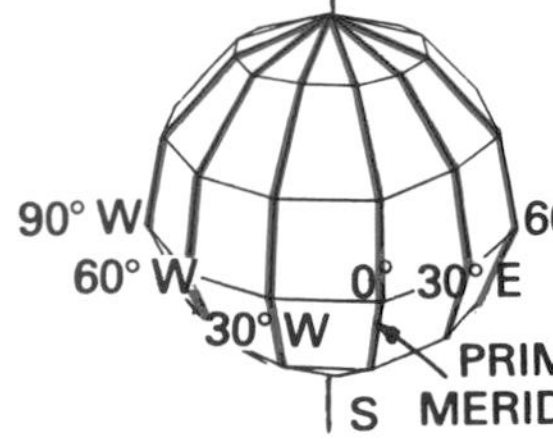

The folds which join the North and South Poles are called meridians or circles of longitude. Once again they are 12 sided polygons on our globe. The 0° meridian is called the Prime Meridian and passes through Greenwich. The other folds are at 30° intervals, east and west.

If you count round in 30° steps you will find that 180°E is the same as 180°W. This is the meridian directly opposite Greenwich.

All meridians have the same diameter as the Equator and the centre of each circle of longitude is the centre of the Earth.

HOW HIGH DO JETS FLY ?

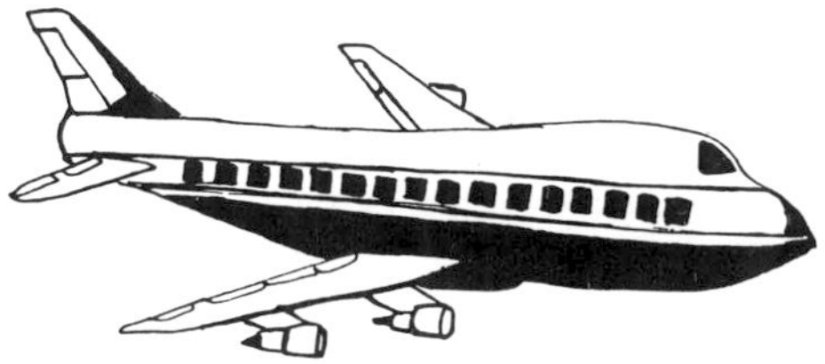

Modern jets climb very rapidly away from the ground as soon as they have taken off. They quickly pass through any cloud into the clear air above and then level off at cruising heights usually between 31,000ft and 39,000ft. (heights of aircraft are almost always given in feet).

How does this compare with the thickness of your paper layer?

Well, 7.5 miles (13km) is about 40,000ft, so almost all commercial flights take place within the layer represented by the paper. We must of course not be too surprised that they fly within the air layer because they need air both for the engines and for lift for the wings.

At the height at which they fly the air is too thin for humans to breathe and so all planes are pressurised. In case there is an accident and the pressurised air inside escapes, there are emergency oxygen supplies for each passenger and each member of the crew. One advantage in flying so high is that it needs less fuel to push the plane through the thin air. The other great advantage is that they are far above bad weather, storms and poor visibility.

HOW HIGH DO ROCKETS FLY ?

Although both planes and rockets fly, their characteristics are very different. Rockets make no use of the air layer because the oxygen they require is carried as part of the fuel. With this restriction removed they can travel out into empty space. There is no limit on the height a rocket can reach or the distance it can fly except that it needs to use enormous quantities of fuel to reach the required speed. If it can go fast enough, then a rocket can leave the Earth permanently. The 'escape velocity' for the Earth is about 25,000mph (40,000kph) and once a rocket has attained that speed, the engines can be switched off and it will never fall back to Earth.

Your globe can also give the impression of what it is like to voyage out into space. Using the scale of 1030 miles to the inch or 650 kilometres to the centimetre, you can find out how far away you have to stand to look back at your globe as if from a satellite, Mars, Venus or the other planets. How far away would be the nearest star?

HOW MUCH SEA AND LAND ?

A visitor from outer space approaching our planet could not fail to notice that there is more than twice as much sea as land. Perhaps you commented on this proportion as you made up and examined your globe. In fact, 71% of the Earth's surface is covered by sea and 29% by land. The Pacific Ocean covers about one third of the whole area of the Earth and you can hold your globe so that almost your whole field of view is sea. Only on the far edge can you see the land of Australia, New Zealand and the Americas. This is a fine example of how a globe gives a much more realistic impression of the real world than a map.

HOW MUCH AIR AND WATER ?

As our planet spins its way through almost empty space, it carries with it a multitude of life forms apart from ourselves. All depend on air and water. Plants, animals, birds, fishes, insects and bacteria are all life forms and all have some need for air and water.

How thick is the layer that can support life?

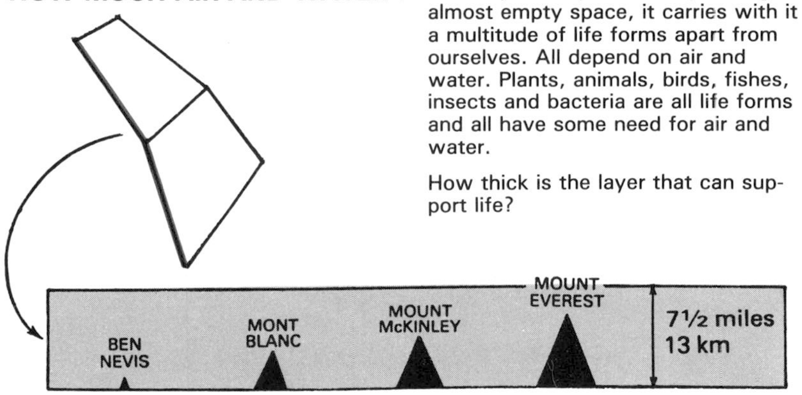

On the scale of your globe, the thickness of the paper represents a layer 7.5 miles (13km) thick. If you place the 'air and water measure' flat on the globe, then most of the air on our planet is within that layer. Only 15% lies outside.

Within that layer are all the mountains, all the rivers, all the lakes, all the ice caps and almost all the clouds.

The greatest depth of the sea so far discovered is in the Mariannas Trench (at 19°N, 146°E) and even there it is only 6.5 miles (11km) deep, less than the thickness of our layer. Most of the sea is far shallower, the average depth being about 2 miles (3.5km).

Within the thickness represented by the paper layer above and below the surface lies all the water and almost all the air. How fragile, how thin is the layer on which all life as we know it depends. How careful we must be not to damage or pollute it.

HOW DO YOU FIND YOUR OWN LATITUDE ?

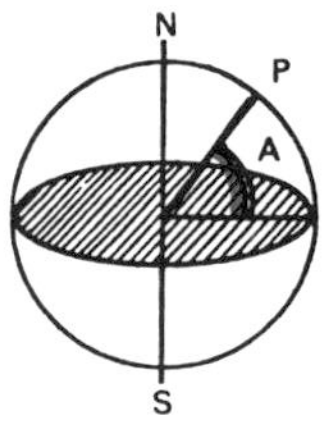

The line joining your position P to the centre of the Earth makes an angle with the plane of the Equator. On the diagram it is marked with an A. A is the angle of latitude.

You can find the latitude of where you live by looking at a map or in the index of an atlas. You can get a rough idea by looking at your globe.

On page 22 there is an interesting practical method to try.

The latitude of London is 51°32′ or approximately 51.5°.

HOW FAR TO THE NORTH POLE ?

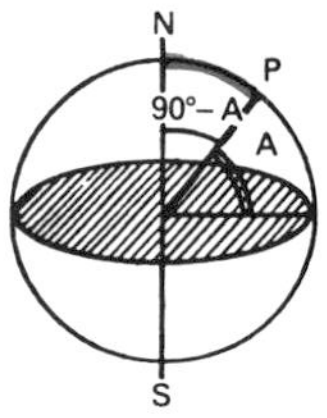

Once you know your latitude this is a very easy calculation. It is a certain fraction of the circumference of the Earth.

The circumference of the Earth is approximately 25,000 miles (40,000km), so the distance to the North Pole is

$\frac{(90-A)}{360} \times 25000$ miles or $\frac{(90-A)}{360} \times 40{,}000$km

For London $90^\circ - A^\circ = 90^\circ - 51.5^\circ = 38.5^\circ$
Hence the distance from London to the North Pole is 2670 miles or 4280km.
You can check this answer with your tape measure. Don't expect a perfect agreement.
What about the Southern Hemisphere ?

WHY GREENWICH ?

While choosing the Equator as the zero for latitude is obvious enough, there is no similar geographical reason for a particular zero for longitude. Until 1884, different countries used different zeros and this was confusing for navigational purposes. Then an International Conference was held in Washington to resolve the matter.

After much discussion, the zero of Britain based on Greenwich was chosen. Britain was then a major sea-faring nation as well as the principal map and chart manufacturer. The meridian through Greenwich became the Prime Meridian of the World and it remains so today.

WHICH WAY IS NORTH ?

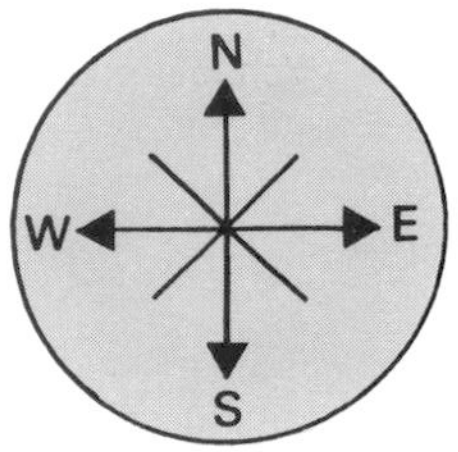

Most people immediately think of using a compass to find north, but this is not as simple as it seems. Magnetic north is not the same as true north. On your globe you will see that the Magnetic North Pole is at present in Northern Greenland and both Magnetic Poles are a long way from the actual Poles. The Earth behaves to some degree as if it were a huge but weak magnet. The truth, however, is rather more complicated. Both Magnetic Poles are slowly moving and there is the added confusion that a compass does not even point directly at them from every position on Earth. There is a considerable variation.

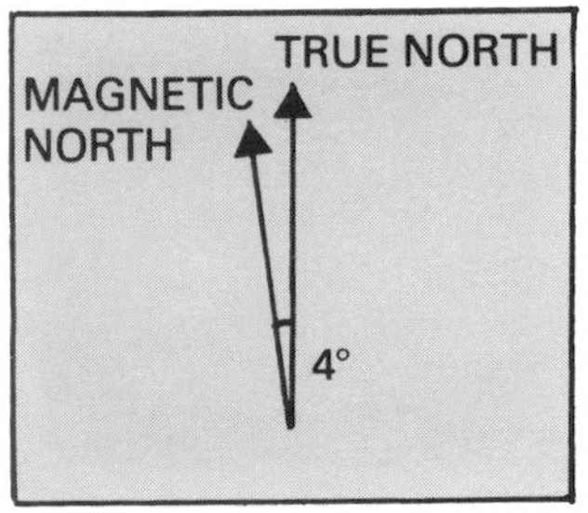

Fortunately at any one place the rate of change of the direction of magnetic north is quite slow. Many large scale maps show the angle by which magnetic north differed from true north on a particular date and indicate the rate of change.

Therefore we can find the direction of true north by using a compass as long as we make the appropriate correction. In England in 1986 the difference is 4° and it is changing at 12′ per year.

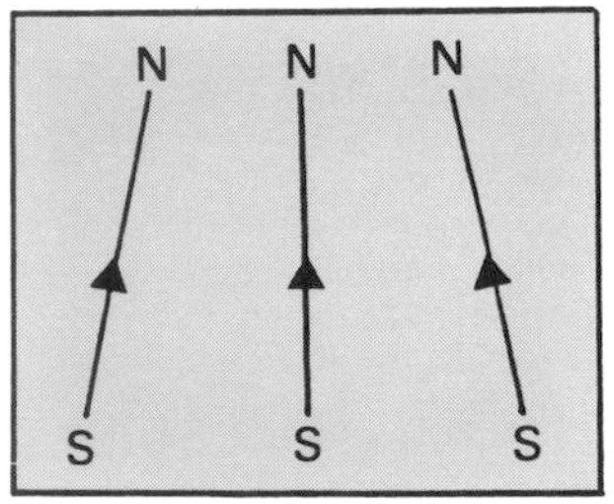

It is easy to make the mistake of thinking that two lines each pointing north must be parallel, because they often look that way on large scale maps.

You can see from your globe that north lines converge on the Poles.

At the North Pole there is no east or west. Every direction you turn, everywhere you look is due south!

WHAT ABOUT THE SUN ?

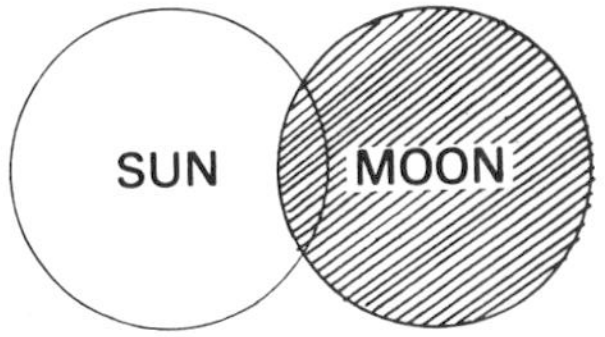

Seen from the Earth, the Sun and the Moon appear to be about the same size. Each subtends half a degree. The Sun is of course much further away and much larger. Occasionally the Moon passes exactly in front of it. Such an event is known as a total eclipse and the Sun's light is blocked out.

Total eclipses do not happen very often, but when they do they are very strange and disturbing experiences. Before the explanation was understood, such a mysterious event was a very frightening one for our ancestors. A total eclipse only lasts for a few minutes, but when it happens it becomes quite dark. If the sky is clear then the stars can be seen. Then the Sun comes out again and the day resumes its normal course. The Moon is of course quite invisible until it crosses the Sun's disc.

Since the Sun is 400 times larger than the Moon and subtends the same angle, it must be about 400 times further away. And so it is. On the scale of your globe it would be a sphere 64ft (20 metres) in diameter, at a distance of 1.4 miles (2.3km).

SOME MODEL !

To make your model of the Earth you had to use 4 sheets of A4 paper.

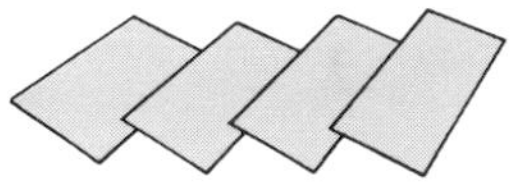

To make a model of the Moon to the same scale, you would need just half of one sheet.

To make a model of the Sun on the same scale as your globe, you would need 40,000 sheets of paper!

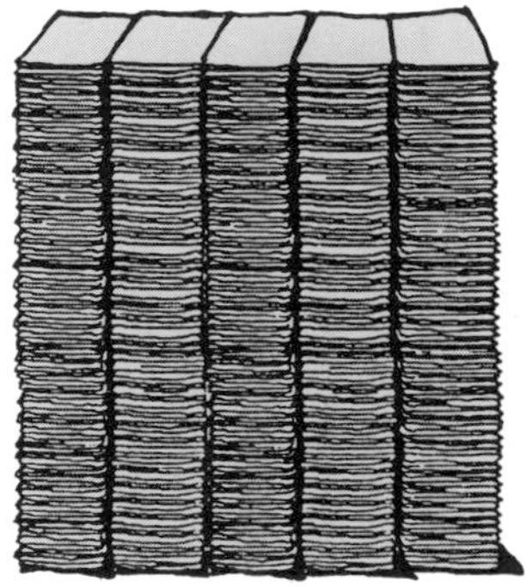

HOW BIG IS THE MOON ?

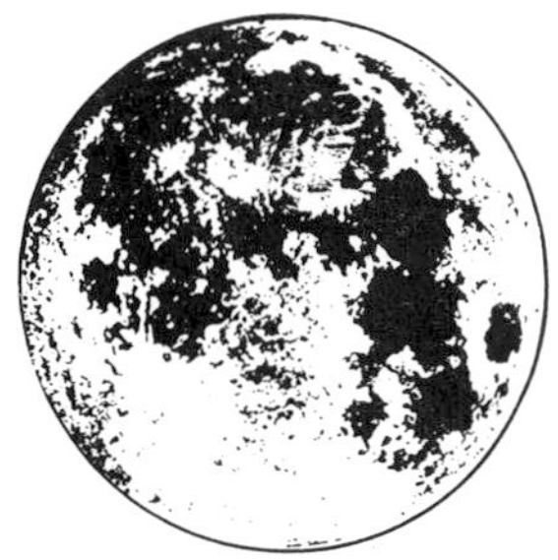

The cut-out of the Full Moon is on the same scale as your globe. The real Moon has a diameter of 2160 miles (3476km), as compared with 7920 miles (12,740km) for the Earth, so that it is roughly one quarter the size.

Although the 'Full Moon' disc is to the scale of the globe and hence is in the correct proportion to its diameter and cross-sectional area, you can get a more vivid impression by comparing volumes. A small apple or tomato with the same cross-section as the cut-out gives a striking demonstration of how much bigger the real Earth is than the real Moon.

HOW FAR AWAY ?

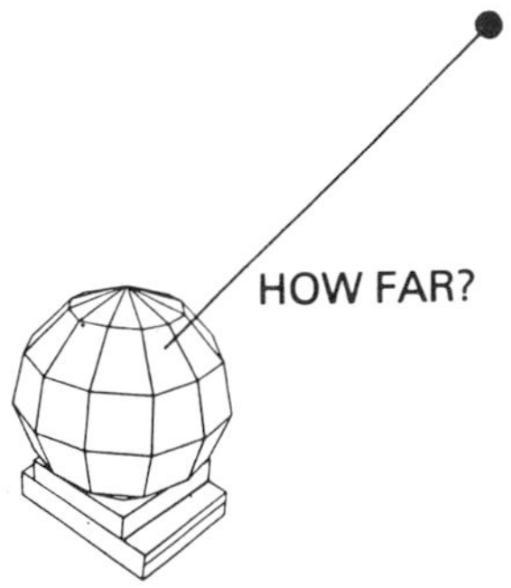

The real Moon is about 239,000 miles (385,000km) from the Earth. It is interesting to ask people to hold the Full Moon disc at what they think is the correct distance from the globe, working to the proper scale.

Most people will hold it far too close. It should be 19 feet or nearly 6 metres away. Take the disc or a correctly sized apple or tomato that distance away and look back at your globe. Then you will see how the Earth looked to the astronauts who landed on the Moon. We can then realize just as they did how remarkably empty space is. We can also be impressed, looking back at the Earth, that the Moon at that distance is still able to cause tides twice each day in the Oceans of the World.

THE HIDDEN SIDE

Just as the Moon causes tides on the Earth, so the Earth has a tidal effect on the Moon. The result has been that the Earth has 'captured' the rotation of the Moon, so that it always presents the same face to the Earth. Because the Moon's orbit is elliptical and not in the equatorial plane, it is possible to see 59% of its surface, but of course never more than 50% at a time!

The remaining 41% had never been seen until 1959, when Luna 3 brought back the first pictures of the far side. During the 1960's and 1970's spacecrafts and astronauts brought back further pictures and the whole surface has now been mapped. Mapped it may be, but the hidden side remains hidden, just as it has been since long before there were human beings on Earth.

HOW CAN WE FIND OUR LONGITUDE ?

LOMELA RIVER ZAIRE	0.14S	20.45E
LOMOND, LOCH SCOTLAND	56.07N	4.36W
LONDON CANADA	42.58N	81.15W
LONDON ENGLAND	51.32N	0.06W
LONDONDERRY N. IRELAND	55.00N	7.21W
LONG, LOCH SCOTLAND	56.05N	4.52W
LONGA RIVER ANGOLA	16.15S	19.07E
LONG BEACH TOWN U.S.A.	33.57 N	18.15W

Nowadays the easiest way is to look up in the index of an atlas the name of your town or city or one which is nearby. A large scale map would give a more accurate answer still.

It used to be very difficult to find your longitude by observation or experiment. Early sailors had great problems and a huge prize was offered for the first person to devise a suitable method. The problem was eventually solved by making a really accurate clock which could be set to Greenwich Mean Time and then be carried on the voyage. The time when the Sun was due south or north was noon local time. Knowing that every 4 minutes of difference between noon local time and noon Greenwich Mean Time is 1° of longitude, it became a simple matter to calculate the ship's position.

From this information you can calculate your own longitude. The BBC World Service broadcasts using Greenwich Mean Time and the 'pips' will allow you to set your watch. You are then ready to observe the time difference between your local noon and GMT and hence calculate your longitude.

HOW CAN WE FIND PLACES ON THE GLOBE ?

If we know the latitude and longitude of a place we want to find, then it is an easy matter to find it. The folds on the globe are at 30° intervals, both for latitude and longitude. You can turn the globe and look on the right surface, and that will probably be enough for you to spot it.

Certain places are virtually on the folds, and are especially easy to find.

New Orleans (30°N, 90°W) Hangchow (30°N, 120°E)

Anchorage (60°N, 150°W)

For other places you can guess roughly the proportion of the way across the 30° intervals.

Here are some places to find.

Kashgar (39°N, 76°E) Dallas (33°N, 97°W)

Auckland (37°S, 175°E) Mexico City (19°N, 99°W)

Nairobi (1°S, 36°E) Seoul (37°N, 127°E)

WHAT IS A GREAT CIRCLE ?

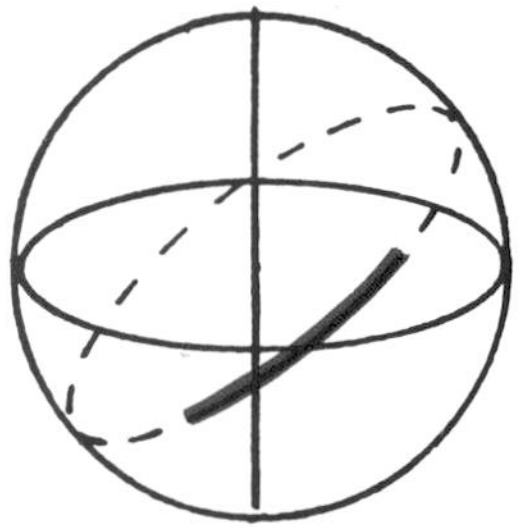

The shortest way between any two points on the surface of the Earth is by what is called the great circle route. If you pull a cord or the distance tape measure tightly across your globe then it will follow the great circle route. Of course you will not get a perfect result because the globe is not a perfect sphere, but it will give a good indication. All great circles have a circumference of approximately 25,000 miles (40,000km) like the Equator and the meridians.

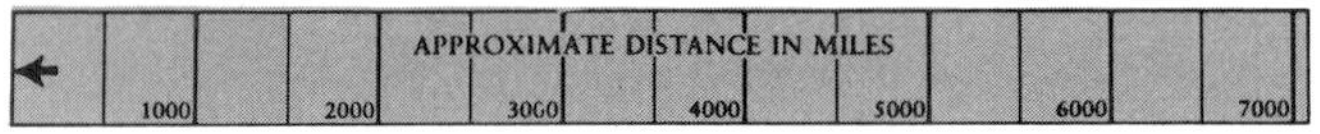

The distance tape measure gives the approximate distance between places anywhere on the globe. On one side the distance is measured in miles, on the other in kilometres.

To measure longer distances and to trace great circle routes, it is a good idea to use a piece of white string. Mark it with units of 500 and 1000 miles or kilometres whichever you prefer.

HOW DO YOU FLY FROM LONDON TO LOS ANGELES ?

London is at 51.5°N, 0°W and Los Angeles is 34°N, 118°W.

Los Angeles is to the south and west of London. It is interesting to find the best route to fly between them using your globe. Pull a piece of string tautly between the two places, or use your distance tape measure.

You might expect to set off to the south-west and thus fly over Cornwall or Brittany. This is not the case! Your best route is to go northwards over Scotland, Greenland and Northern Canada. That this is the shortest route is beyond doubt, but it is still impressive to leave London on a summer day bound for the heat of Southern California and yet see beneath the plane the icebergs, glaciers and snowfields of Greenland.

WHEREVER DID THURSDAY GO?

MON.	TUES.	WED.	FRI.	SAT.
12	13	14	16	17

An American University Professor was invited to give a special commemoration lecture on Thursday 15th May at 3.00pm in Melbourne, Australia. He left San Francisco at 11.00 p.m. on Wednesday 14th May for a 13 hour flight to Melbourne.Thirteen hours later he arrived at noon next day San Francisco Time, which was 6.00 a.m. Melbourne time and he adjusted his watch.

It was too early in the morning for the reception committee to meet him, so he went to the airport restaurant for breakfast. When no-one had arrived by 9.00 a.m. he began to be rather puzzled. It was then that he realised that it was Friday morning and that he had completely missed the lecture!

Wherever did Thursday go? You can check all this on your globe with the time collar. Where was he when the lecture should have started?

IT IS TOMORROW TODAY !

A problem with a missing day occurred on the very first circumnavigation of the globe by Magellan. Having sailed westward past South America through what is now called the Straits of Magellan, they sailed westward across the Pacific. Magellan himself was killed, but the ship continued westward round South Africa and made landfall in the Cape Verde Islands (17°N,25°W) on Wednesday 9th July 1522. Or rather that was the day they thought it was. The inhabitants thought it was Thurday 10th July and of course neither was wrong. Or were they? In those days there was no International Date Line, so where did the extra day come from or go to?

WHO IS REALLY OLDER ?

"MY TWIN BROTHER'S BIRTHDAY WAS YESTERDAY AND MINE IS TODAY. I WAS BORN FIRST, SO I AM OLDER"

On an ocean liner sailing east across the Date Line, a woman gave birth to twins. The first, Peter was born on Wednesday 11th October and a little later that same morning the second, Paul was born on Tuesday 10th October.

When they came to celebrate their birthdays in later years, Paul had his party on October 10th. Peter had his on the next day October 11th.

Peter always said that he was really older than his brother, but no-one would believe him. Was he really?

WHAT IS THE INTERNATIONAL DATE LINE ?

There is one problem with time which most of us are unaware of. Your globe will help you to understand it.

Set your time collar so that it is 6.00 p.m. on the Greenwich Meridian. Let us assume that it is Tuesday.

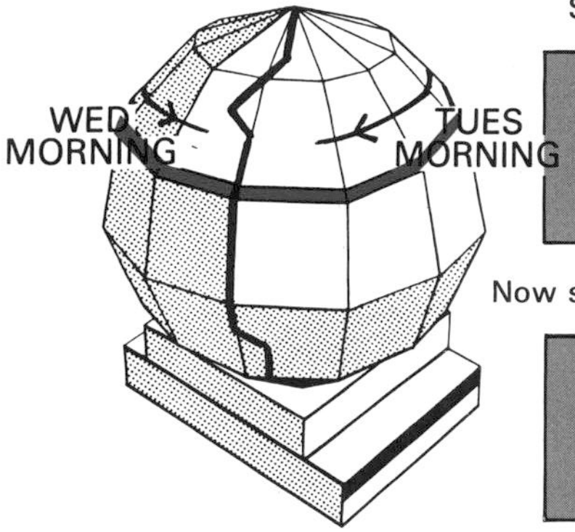

Start at Greenwich and go eastwards

In England it is 6.00 p.m. Tuesday evening.
In Saudi-Arabia it is 9.00 p.m. Tuesday evening.
In India it is 11.00 p.m. Tuesday evening.
In Thailand it is 1.00 a.m. Wednesday morning.
In the Kiribati Islands it is 5.40 a.m. Wednesday morning.

Now start again at Greenwich and go westwards.

In England it is 6.00 p.m. Tuesday evening.
In Mexico it is 11.00 a.m. Tuesday morning.
In California it is 10.00 a.m. Tuesday morning.
In Hawaii it is 7.30 a.m. Tuesday morning.
In the Howard and Baker Islands it is about 6.30 a.m. on Tuesday morning.

Between the Kiribati Islands and the Howard and Baker Islands lies the International Date Line. on the left side it is early Wednesday morning, on the right side it is early Tuesday morning. There is a sudden jump of a complete day as you cross the line.

If you are travelling eastwards, you will find that

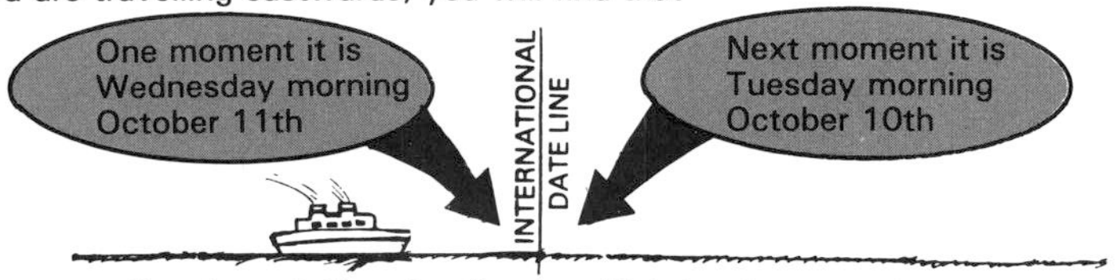

and you can live through Tuesday October 10th for the second time!

If you are travelling westwards, you will find that

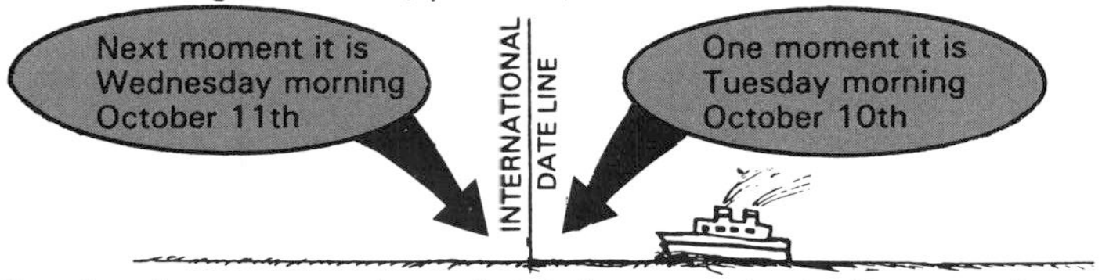

and Tuesday afternoon, evening and night have completely disappeared!

HOW FAST ARE YOU MOVING ?

Unless you are reading this while actually travelling, you might be tempted to think that you were not moving at all. But of course you are. You are a passenger on Spaceship Earth as it rotates about its axis and moves in its orbit around the Sun.

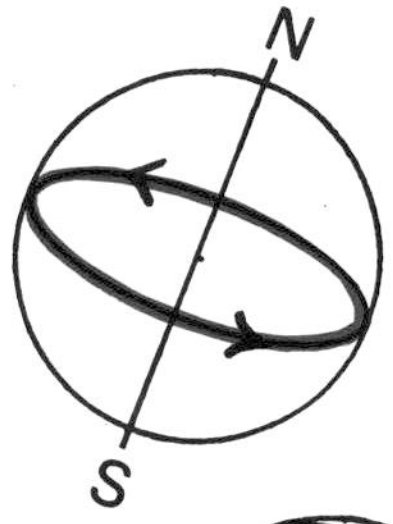

If you lived exactly on the Equator you would move round a circle equivalent in length to the Equator each day.The Equator is approximately 25,000 miles (40,000km) long and so your speed is 1040 mph or 1670 kph.

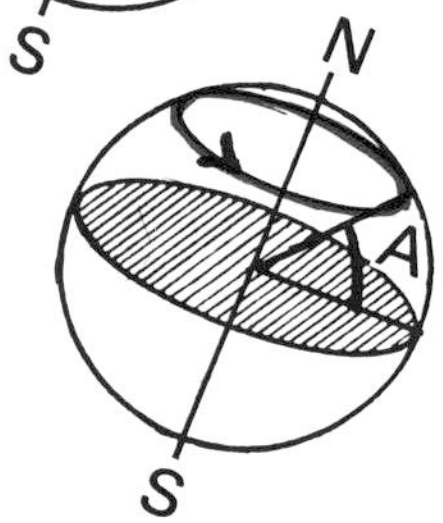

At a higher latitude either north or south, the circumference of the circle you cover each day is rather smaller. Its length depends on the Cosine of A, your angle of latitude, as does your speed.

Your speed is 1040 CosA mph or 1670 CosA kph.

In London A = 51.5°, and so if you live in or near London your speed is 647 mph or 1040 kph.

At both the North and South Poles you would not move at all. You would just rotate once in every 24 hours.

WHAT IS THE ECLIPTIC ?

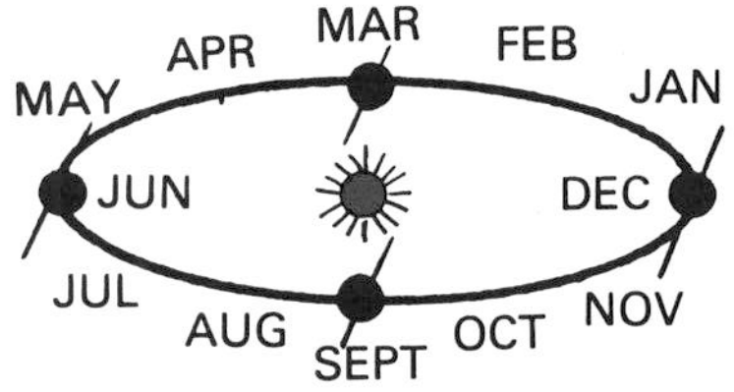

The Earth travels through space around the Sun, taking one year to complete the orbit. The plane in which it travels is called the 'The Plane of the Ecliptic'.

Do not be led astray by the scale of this sketch. See page 18.

The Earth is also moving in its orbit around the Sun at an average speed of about 67,000 mph (107,000 kph).

Working to the scale of your globe it means that in a normal school lesson of 35 or 40 minutes, your globe would move about 3 or 4 feet - say roughly a metre.In the same lesson, the real Earth takes you,the school buildings and everyone else, on a journey of 44,000 miles (70,000km).

WHAT MAKES DAY AND NIGHT ?

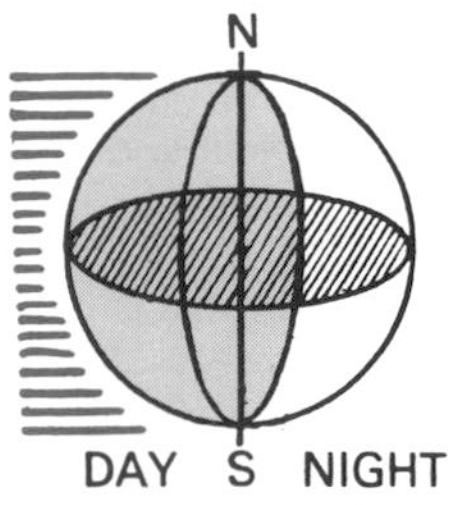

THE SITUATION ON
MAR 21 AND SEPT 21

It is the rotation of the Earth which brings us into and out of the Sun's rays and causes the alternation of day and night. Although half of the Earth's surface is always bathed in sunlight, this does not mean that individual places have exactly 12 hours day and 12 hours night. Because of the tilt of the axis, equal days and nights only occur twice a year, on 21st March and 21st September. At other times of year the division between day and night depends on the exact date and the latitude.

Each morning we are carried round from the shadow into the sunlight and we see the Sun appear above the horizon in the east. Not the exact east of course, because that also depends on the date and the latitude, but on the eastward side of the horizon. As the Earth's rotation carries us round more and more under the direct rays of the Sun, we see the Sun appear to rise in the sky until it reaches the highest point for that day. That is the time we call noon. As the day continues we are gradually carried round out of the Sun's rays so that it appears to set in the west. Not of course the exact west, that direction also depends on the date and the latitude!

The Sun crosses the sky in different directions in the two hemispheres.

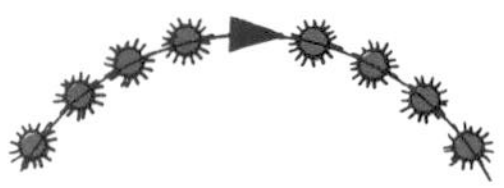

North of latitude 23.5°N the Sun crosses the sky each day from left to right.

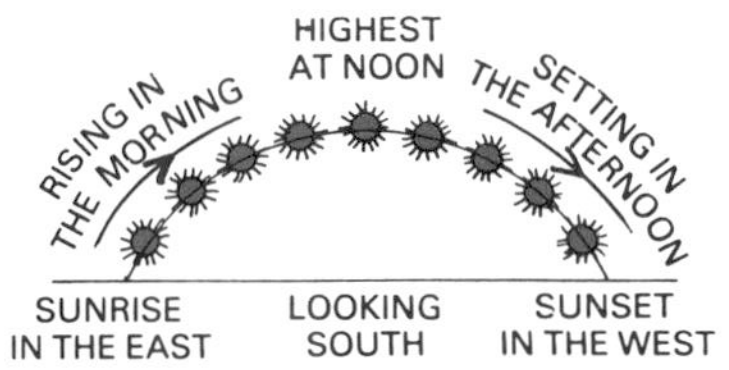

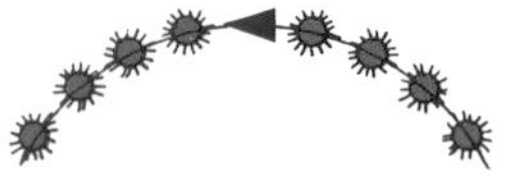

South of latitude 23.5°S the Sun crosses the sky from right to left.

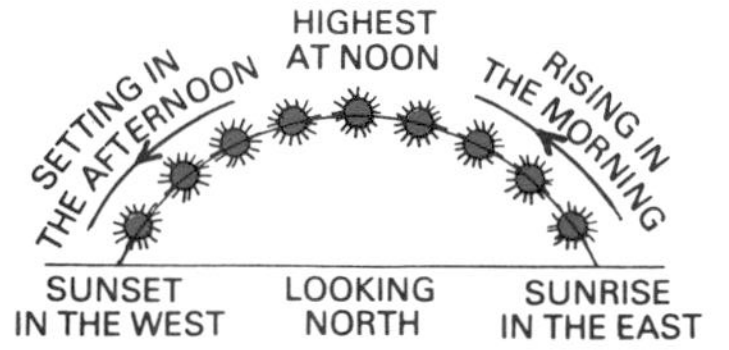

To understand why the latitudes of 23.5°N and 23.5°S are important and what happens between them, we have now to consider the orbit of the Earth round the Sun.

WHAT IS JET LAG ?

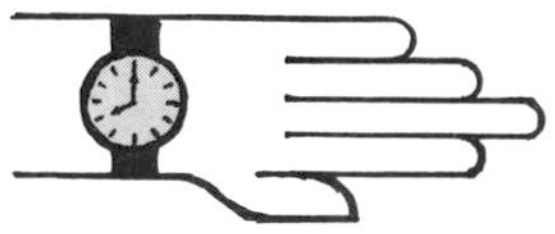

HIS WATCH SHOWS THE TIME
AS 8 O'CLOCK

Jets can fly very quickly and at high latitudes as fast as the Earth rotates.

You can leave London at 1.00 p.m. fly the Atlantic for 7 hours and then arrive in the U.S.A. where it is 3.00 p.m.. Your watch says it is 8.00 p.m., but the clocks in the airport say 3.00 p.m. It is mid-afternoon, not evening.
The sunlight tells you so.

Four hours after your arrival, you feel that it is midnight. For everyone around you it is only 7.00 p.m. and they are just about to go out for the evening.The strange, confused feeling which people suffer from is called 'jet-lag'.

Jet lag is a thoroughly unpleasant experience for most people. The human body gets accustomed to the normal rhythms of activity and the sudden change to a different time zone upsets the body clock. People find that they wake in the middle of the night thinking that it is morning and then drop off to sleep during the day. They may not feel hungry at mealtimes, but become ravenous later. It takes most people about one day for each hour of change before the body comes back into a stable rhythm again.

Of course a seven hour flight from Europe to Africa or from North to South America does not produce this effect. You may feel tired from the journey, but your body clock remains correctly set.

USING YOUR JUMBO JET TAPE MEASURE

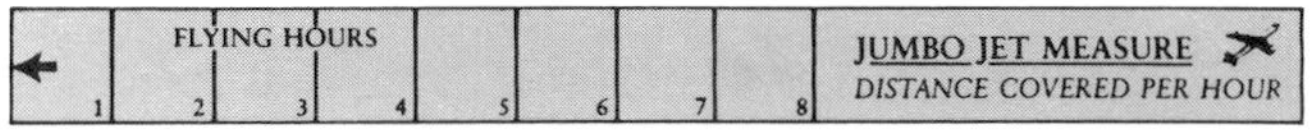

Use the tape measure to see how far you can go in a given time travelling at the normal cruising speed of a jumbo jet. Where can you fly to in 7 hours? At what latitude does the time change by 2 hours for 2 hours flying?

USING YOUR OCEAN LINER TAPE MEASURE

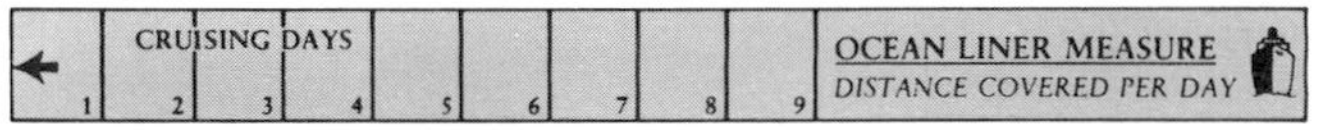

An ocean liner can sail as far as 500 miles (800km) in a day. Most cruising is done in warmer climates near to the Equator, where even sailing due east or west produces a time change of less than 30 minutes a day. This is an amount of time-change your body can easily cope with. People may well suffer from sea-sickness on liners but no-one suffers from 'liner-lag'.

WORLD TIME ZONES

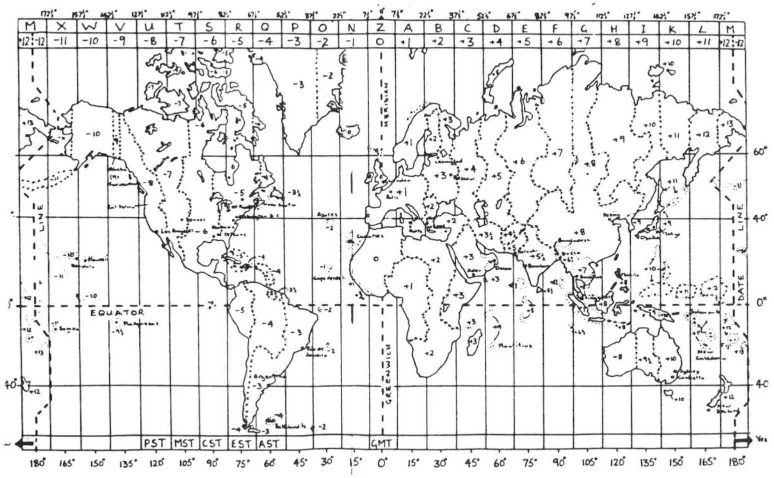

The map above, using Mercator's projection shows the 24 time zones into which the world has been divided. It also shows the times which people actually use, which are not always the same. Why is there a difference?

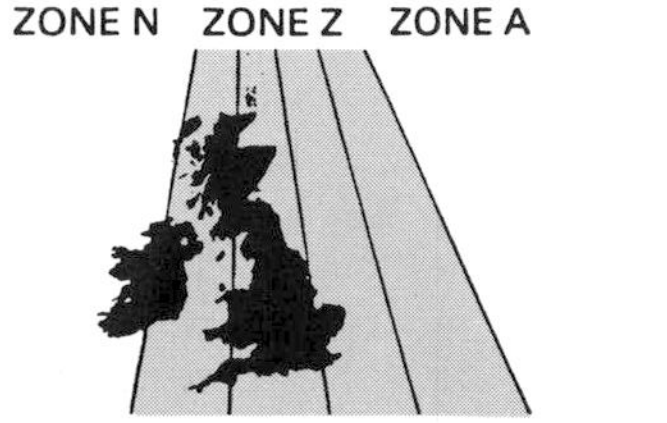

Although most of Britain and Ireland falls within the same time zone, the far west of Ireland does not. When it is 3.15 p.m. on one side of the line it should be 2.15 p.m. on the other. This would be most inconvenient for people living there, so all of Ireland uses Greenwich Mean Time.

In countries like the U.S.A. or Russia, the differences are too great to do this. Between New York and San Francisco there is a difference of 194 minutes. The practical time zones still do not change on the theoretical line, but on convenient state or province boundaries. China is the most notable exception, keeping Peking Time over the whole country.

SUMMER TIME

In order to save fuel and to make the best use of daylight most countries put their clocks forward or backwards for some period of the year. Britain uses GMT during the winter and puts its clocks forward during the summer. Other countries do similarly, often changing on different dates. If you want to know exactly what the official time is in a particular country, you can find out from the International Telephone Operator.

WHAT MAKES SUMMER AND WINTER ?

The orbit around the Sun is not a perfect circle, but an ellipse. However it is not the change of distance of the Earth from the Sun which causes summer and winter.(The Earth is actually closest to the Sun in January, when it is winter in the northern hemisphere.)The reason is that the plane of the Equator is tilted at 23.5° to the plane of the ecliptic.

The Sun's rays fall more directly on the northern hemisphere and it is summer there.It is winter in the southern hemisphere.

The Sun's rays fall more directly on the southern hemisphere and it is summer there.It is winter in the northern hemisphere.

In the diagram above we are looking as if from outer space. How does it appear from our viewpoint on Earth? As the Sun's rays fall more directly on our part of the Earth,we see the Sun appearing higher in the sky. The higher the Sun is in the sky, the more energy arrives on each unit of area and the warmer it is, neglecting the effects of clouds and weather.

WHERE IS THE SUN DIRECTLY OVERHEAD ?

It will be hottest when the Sun is highest in the sky, and it cannot be higher than directly overhead! Many people think that this only occurs on the Equator, but this is not the case. On the Equator, the Sun is only directly overhead at noon on the 21st March and 21st September.

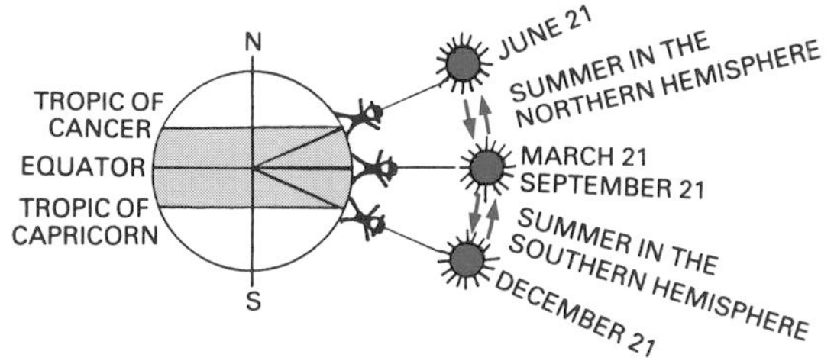

Because of the tilt of the axis, the Sun is directly overhead on two days a year at all latitudes between 23.5°N(The Tropic of Cancer) and 23.5°S (The Tropic of Capricorn). Between the tropics the Sun will be to the north or south at different times of the year. The Sun will always be high in the sky at noon and it will always be warm, hence the word 'tropical'.

WHAT IS THE MAXIMUM ELEVATION OF THE SUN ?

In summer the Sun rises to a greater elevation at noon than it does in the winter and remains above the horizon for longer. The actual path of the Sun through the sky is different every day because it depends on the orbit, the rotation and the tilt and it is not easy to calculate. However, it is easy to calculate the maximum and minimum noon values for any latitude.

Outside the tropics, the angle of elevation of the Sun is at the maximum of the year at noon on Midsummer Day.

It is (90°-latitude) + 23.5°
For London, which is 51.5°N
it is (90-51.5) + 23.5 = 62°

At noon on Midwinter Day, the angle of elevation of the Sun is at the minimum noon elevation of the year.
It is (90°-latitude) - 23.5°
For London it is (90-51.5) - 23.5 = 15°

WHAT IS THE MIDNIGHT SUN ?

On your globe you will see dotted lines at 66.5°N and 66.5°S which are the Arctic and Antarctic Circles. Within those circles the tilt of the Earth's axis produces other effects which may seem very curious to those of us who do not live there.

Let us calculate the elevation of the Sun at noon on Midwinter Day It is (90°-67.5°)-23.5° = 0°

So the Sun does not rise above the horizon at all. It is still night in the middle of the day!

Nearer to the Poles the Sun does not rise for several weeks around Midwinter Day and the night is unbroken.

During the summer the position is reversed and there is a period of unbroken day. The Sun passes round the horizon day after day, rising to a maximum in the south at noon and falling to a minimum in the north at midnight. This is the 'Midnight Sun'.

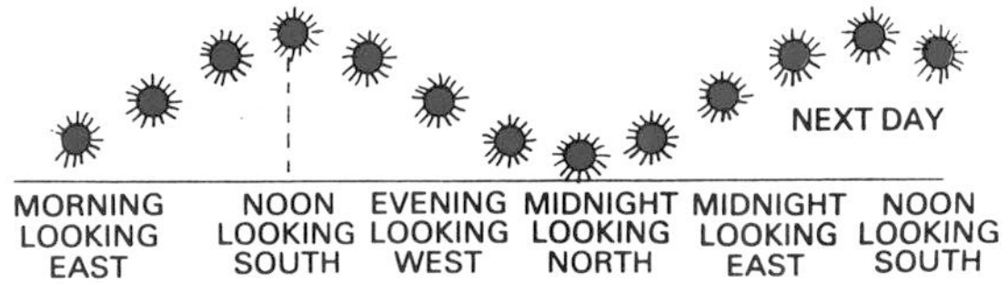

What would this diagram be like, viewed from the actual Poles themselves?

WHAT IS LOCAL TIME ?

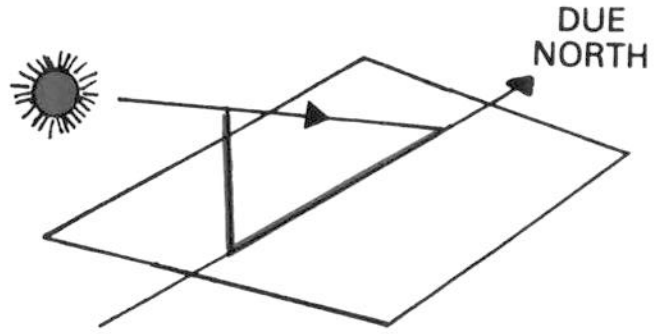

Local time is the natural or 'sundial time' measured by the motion of the Sun across the sky. The interval from local noon to local noon next day is divided into 24 equal hours. Local noon is the instant when the Sun is highest in the sky at that particular location. It is also the time, north of the Tropic of Cancer, when the Sun is due south and the shadow of a vertical stick points due north. South of the Tropic of Capricorn the position is reversed. The Sun is due north and the shadow points due south.

THE TIME COLLAR

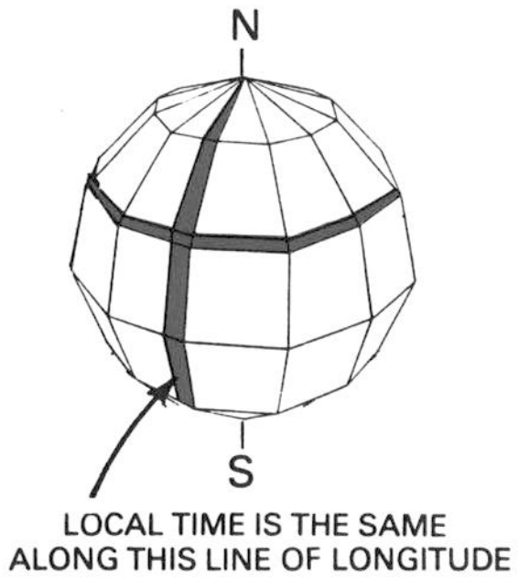

The fold lines on your globe are at 30° intervals and so the local time differs by 2 hours at each division. We can use the cut-out time collar to show what the local time is anywhere in the world at the present moment. Simply adjust the collar until the line of longitude through where you live shows the current local time. Then you can look and see what time it is everywhere around the Earth.

Remember that the time is the same along the complete half circle of longitude. Time is different from east to west, but not from north to south.

WHAT IS ZONE TIME ?

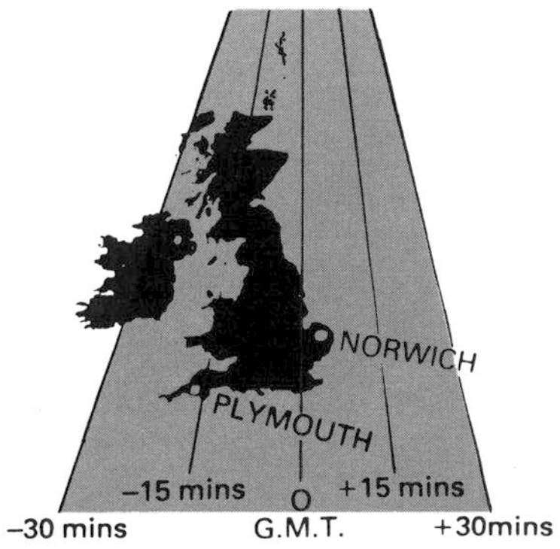

The use of local time would cause plenty of problems even in a country as small as England.

If each place used its own time, then a traveller would have to keep altering his watch. The passengers on a train between London and Norwich would have to put their watches forward by 5 minutes on arrival in Norwich and back by 5 minutes on arrival in London. Between London and Plymouth the difference would be 16 minutes. Imagine trying to make train connections if the railways used local time!
The solution to the problem is for all places 7.5° either side of the Meridian to use Meridian time. The Sun is highest in the sky at 11.55 a.m.in Norwich or 12.16 p.m. in Plymouth, but no-one notices.

The whole world has been divided into 24 time zones.

34

33

34 34

30

33

30

32 32

31 31 H

28

28 28

H G

28 28

28 26 28

28

28

H

THE GLOBE SECTION 4

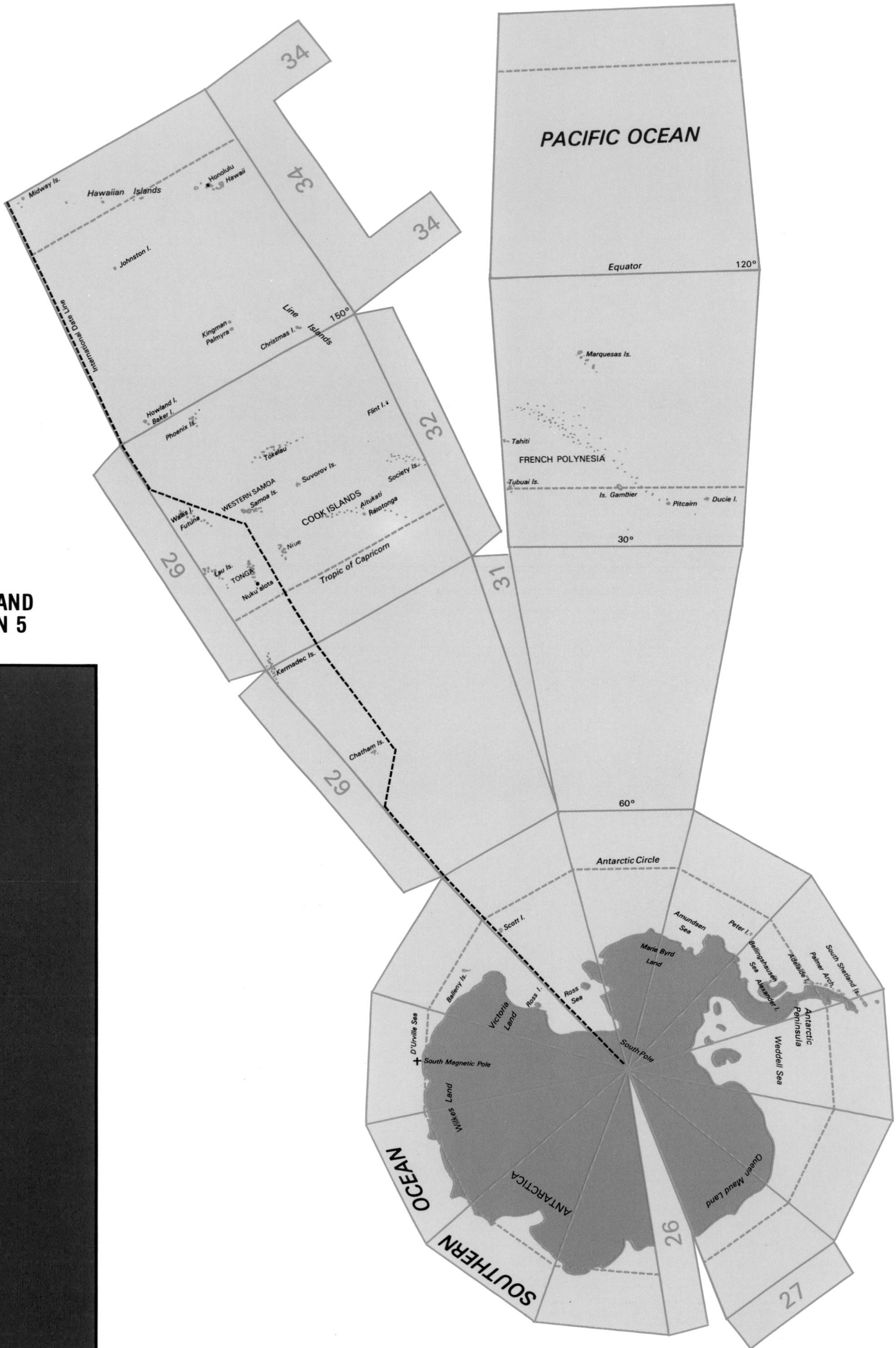

THE STAND
SECTION 5

THE STAND SECTION 1 SEE OVER

D

A A

A A

D

THE STAND SECTION 1

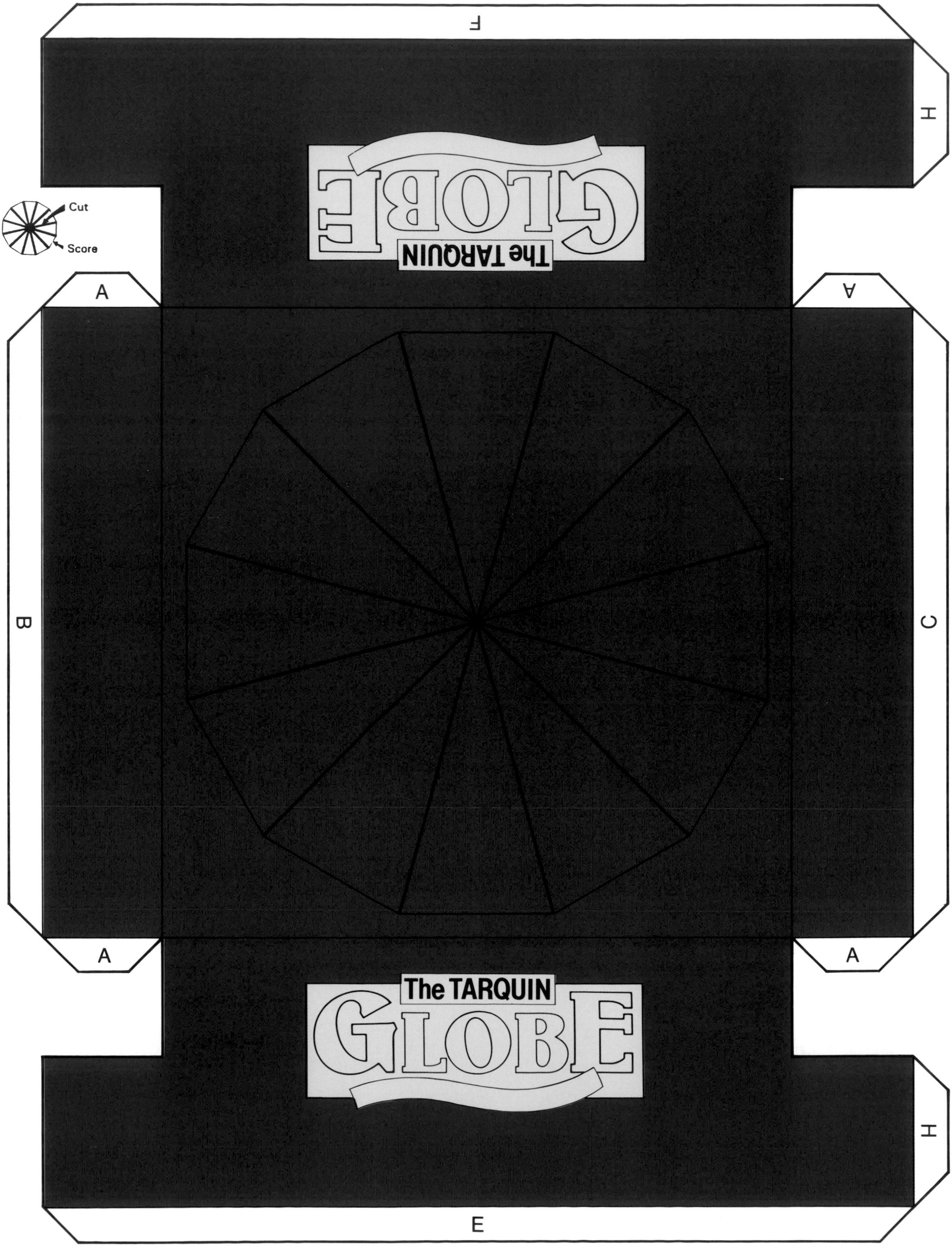

F

E

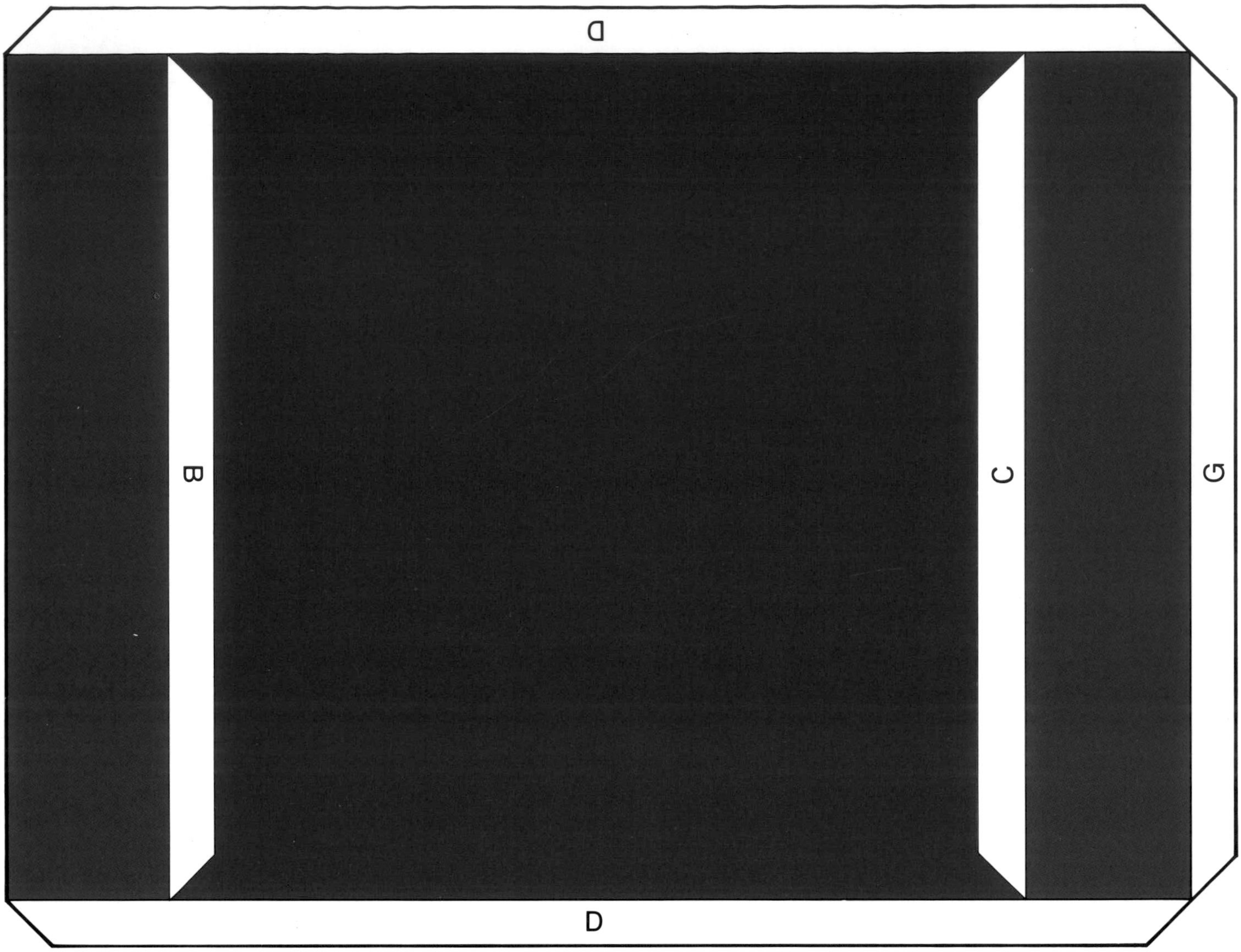
D
B
C
G
D

H